THE TERRACE
An Educational Experiment in a State School

By the same author
Work, Language and Education in the Industrial State (1991)

FREEDOM PRESS publish *Freedom* (fortnightly) and *The Raven* (quarterly) as well as books (more than sixty titles in print)

FREEDOM PRESS BOOKSHOP carries the most comprehensive stock of anarchist literature, including titles from North America. Please send for our current list.

**Freedom Press
in Angel Alley
84b Whitechapel High Street
London
E1 7QX**

The Terrace

An Educational Experiment in a State School

Michael Duane

with a Foreword
by
Colin Ward

FREEDOM PRESS
London
1995

Published by
FREEDOM PRESS
84b Whitechapel High Street
London
E1 7QX
1995

© Michael Duane, Colin Ward and Freedom Press

ISBN 0 900384 78 6

Contents

Foreword
by Colin Ward   7

Acknowledgements   14

Introduction   15

Part I
Origins of the Conisbrough Experiment   23

Part II
ROSLA I (1973-74)
The First Term   29

Part III
ROSLA I (1973-74)
Dialogue with Dave   45

Part IV
Some Evidence and Some Conclusions   63

'If, in therapy, it is possible to rely upon the capacity of the client to deal constructively with his life situation and if the therapist's aim is best directed towards releasing that capacity, then why not apply this hypothesis and this method in teaching? If the creation of an atmosphere of acceptance, understanding and respect is the most effective basis for facilitating the learning which we call therapy, then might it not be the basis for the learning which is called education? If the outcome of this approach to therapy is a person who is not only better informed in regard to himself, but who is better able to guide himself intelligently in new situations, might a similar outcome be hoped for in education?'

Carl Rogers, 'Student-Centred Teaching' in *Client-Centred Therapy*, Constable, 1951.

★ ★ ★

Dave: You can't have a Dartington up in Conisbrough.

DK: Why not?

Dave: Cause it's wrong area for it. It's *environment*, environment round here. You can't have a Dartington Hall School *here, can* you?

MD: Why?

Dave: You just *can't*! It's two different things!

MD: Is it the area or the money or the parents or the habits of the kids or the habits of the teachers or the equipment of the school -- which of these things?

Dave: Every one! It's money, it's everything! I mean, there isn't a lot of people round here wi a lot of money cause it's a working-class area, in't it!

MD: It's a different attitude to life, is it?

Dave (emphatically): Yeh!

Foreword

The publicly-funded school system in Britain has, since 1980, been subjected to a counter-revolution, even though the revolution that is being suppressed never actually happened.

Before 1979 primary and secondary schools, and further education colleges, were the responsibility of local education authorities and their budgets were controlled by these bodies, mostly through grants from central government (because of its virtual monopoly of revenue-gathering). The monitoring of standards in schools was conducted by Her Majesty's Inspectorate, a high-prestige body whose members liked to boast that it was completely independent of, and a great deal older than, the government ministry, the Department of Education and Science.

Since 1979 there has been unremitting pressure from central government to wrest control of schools away from local authorities and into the hands of central government.

In part this can be seen as a plot by top civil servants who, at last, found a government willing to centralise control, while using the empty rhetoric of advancing parental choice. Some observers conclude that Conservative governments have been snared by their own faith, firstly in the free-market pressure groups, persuading them that schooling is a commodity to be bought in the cheapest market; secondly by the Treasury, finding that the biggest educational expense is that of hiring teachers; and thirdly by the intense campaign of upper-level (privately-educated) civil servants, to gain control of the school system. There is evidence for this point of view in a careful study by John Dunford of this struggle for control.[1]

Others see the control of schools as an aspect (as in the case of housing) of the war of attrition by central government against local government. Schools have been encouraged to 'opt out' of council control and accept more generous direct funding from government. These decisions may not imply approval of current government policy. I know of schools which have 'opted out' to avoid the selection-at-eleven-plus policies of their Conservative county council, or to secure their survival in the case of small rural primary schools condemned to closure by their local authorities.

A further aspect of the war against teachers has been the introduction of a National Curriculum and the imposition of testing at various fixed ages. Following non-cooperation by the teachers' unions, these proposals have been endlessly modified, but the political opposition too has given its support to this totalitarian measure. part of the trauma of post-Franco Spain, post-Salazar Portugal and post-Soviet Russia and its empire has been the struggle of teachers to free themselves from a National Curriculum. A minor sad reflection on the National Curriculum notion is the fact that all the subjects in it are taught everywhere anyway. We already had a depressing uniformity in education.

The final segment of the Conservative demonology of education was described by Kenneth Clarke, when he was Secretary of State, as the 'half-baked old-fashioned, progressive ideology' seen by our rulers as responsible not only for what they see as a decline in literacy and numeracy in Britain, but for the collapse of manufacturing industry in this country.

If the Secretary of State had been in office long enough to learn the Who's Who of the education world, he would have seen the author of this book, Michael Duane, as a prototype of the ideology he had in mind. He is famous as the head teacher of Risinghill School in North London, which was closed by the London County Council Education Department (later ILEA) without any public discussion of the reasons why. (For a partial account of a partial book on the events see the Freedom Press volume *A Decade of Anarchy*.[2]) Blacklisted for the jobs he applied for, he earned his keep in the teachers' colleges, notably Garnett College, and sought out educational experiments where his insights could be useful. His preoccupations are disclosed in another Freedom Press book, *Work, Language and Education in the Industrial State*.[3]

There he remarked on 'work' that 'The nature of work in industrial society today is such that those who stop to think about it wonder why so many millions of otherwise sane people spend so much of their lives, apparently without complaint, at work over which they have no control and from which they derive no personal satisfaction beyond receiving a wage ...' In today's situation of large-scale, long-term unemployment, the reason is all too clear, but Duane moves on to the issue of language: 'As well as the disparity in income/wealth and political power between the ends of the spectrum of work, there is a third factor of importance. It is the degree to which the various categories of work require the exercise of linguistic skills on the part of the worker for their successful performance ...'

The text before you presents his conclusions in the 1970s, when we still had educational experiments, on a venture exploring both these issues at Conisbrough in South Yorkshire, a place dependent on the coal-mining industry. He visited The Terrace over a period of two years. I spent a week there in 1973, memorable for me as the only time when I have ever been down a mine. Needless to say, twenty years later, all pits in the area have been closed. In a report on the impressions that I gained of the Terrace at the time, I wrote: 'Our impressions of this fully mechanised colliery which employs 1,400 local men and produces over half a million tons of coal a year were like those of any other visitor: the scale of operations and the grim working conditions. The average age of the miners at Cadeby is 48, and no one we met in the entire week, miners, officials or trade union veterans, said that he would encourage his son to go to work in the pit'.[4]

Perceptions of the coal industry have changed dramatically under the Conservative onslaught, and so have perceptions of the education industry. So much so indeed that it may be useful to the reader if I expand on the explanations provided by Michael Duane. Here is a cast of characters for the drama he unfolds:

Educational Priority Areas (EPAs) were recommended in the Plowden Report of 1967,[5] to take the form of 'positive discrimination' for schools in deprived areas of Britain, which might take the form of better staff/student ratios, improved buildings and more money to spend. One of the 31 areas so favoured was Conisbrough, a South Yorkshire town of about 18,000 people. A building there called the Red House became the home of the West Riding EPA project, and Professor A.H. Halsey who reported to the government on the working of EPAs, remarked that 'if I was asked to say which was the single most exciting, most successful experience of the three year project, I would undoubtedly point to the Red House'.[6]

Raising of the School Leaving Age (ROSLA). The raising of the minimum legal age for leaving school to 16 in 1972/3 succeeded EPAs as a focus for educational heart-searching and experiment. If school had become meaningless for a certain proportion of students by the age of 15, what could another year achieve? The venture at The Terrace as an alternative to school was a joint venture by Dartington Hall, the West Riding Education Department and Northcliffe Community High School.

Dartington Hall. This famous experiment in rural reconstruction was started in 1925 when Dorothy and Leonard Elmhirst bought a derelict estate in Devon. She was an American heiress, he was a Yorkshire farmer's son. Both were influenced by the social ideas of Rabindranath Tagore and they initiated a variety of enterprises in agriculture, industry and the arts.[7] The most famous of these was Dartington Hall School, the progressive school which made headlines until its closure in 1987. It had a variety of head teachers, good and bad, the most celebrated of whom was W.B. Curry from 1931 to 1957. Royston Lambert was the head from 1969 to 1973. He wanted to reduce the school's 'isolation from the community' and remarked, 'Frankly I was not prepared to become head of a school solely for the education of the rich. Apart from my own delicate moral scruples on the matter, the conventional English boarding school which operates as a sort of closed ghetto for children of one social, economic and cultural group seemed to me to be profoundly non-educative, confining instead of enlarging the experiences of young people and their awareness of their society and its diverse cultures'.[8] Lambert wanted an exchange between Dartington and an ordinary secondary school, and to provide a base for an alternative school for young people in the 14-16 age range 'who have hitherto been indifferent or antagonistic to their schooling'.[9] In this book Michael Duane provides a detailed account of his proposals.

Sir Alec Clegg. He was Chief Education Officer for the West Riding of Yorkshire. On the centenary of the Education Act of 1870 he gave a lecture on 'The Education of John Robinson', reminding us that the Newsom Report on secondary education[10] had examined the problems faced by children of average and below-average ability.

Foreword

Newsom divided them into John Brown, John Jones and, in the least able quarter of any age range, John Robinson. I will quote at length Clegg's version of Newsom's detailed survey:

'He's the son of an unskilled worker with a large family, living in a poor area. He starts at his secondary school below average in height, weight and measurable intelligence and he's placed in a low stream in the school. He it is who would profit most by a generous use of the school's practical rooms but he is in fact allowed less use of them than either John Brown or John Jones. Though teaching him is one of the hardest jobs, he's often taught by the poorest teachers, and when a teacher is absent it's he who has to make shift. This isn't my invention: all these facts come from a national survey conducted for us when we were on the Newsom Committee. The school isn't concerned about him as it is about those who will bring it the renown of examination successes. He dislikes wearing uniform and is seldom a member of the school society or team. He has free dinners, and although Newsom didn't point this out, he often has to queue for his ticket after those who pay have received theirs. He who most needs the spur of success rarely experiences it. He lacks that most powerful of all educational forces, the parental aspiration which does so much for the middle-class child, and he lacks what HMIs described over 100 years ago as "that recognition which our natures crave and acknowledge with renewed endeavour".'

At this point Alec Clegg has us all nodding with agreement. Yes, we all knew John Robinson. So he added his most devastating comment:

'Now may I continue where Newsom left off? He leaves school as soon as he can but is often among the last to land a job, and when he does land one it doesn't carry the distinction of day-release or an apprenticeship; and as he's virtually discarded by his school, he avoids the youth club and further education, both of which remind him of it. He knows the misery of unimportance: and as no teacher has ever been a John Robinson, no teacher knows the depth of his resentment.'[11]

It is easy to understand why Clegg welcomed the Dartington proposal.

Arthur Young and Northcliffe School. I had a surprise when I first visited this school. Like many another school building of seventy or eighty years ago, it had two quadrangles surrounded by classrooms. But, unlike any other school I had seen, these quadrangles had been turned into something between a menagerie and a farm. There were cocks and hens, ducks and drakes, guinea fowl, guinea pigs and rabbits, a peacock and peahen and their egg, and even a mynah bird responding to my queries in a South Yorkshire accent. I knew that the head, while under the constraints legally applicable to any head teacher, must be an unusual person, and he was. Arthur Young had for many years been trying to find the right equation between learning and earning. He remarked of work experience projects that they 'have never really got off the ground because of the legal, insurance and trade union problems that hedge them around. I have always thought that the schemes proposed were phoney – the most important aspect of work experience being neglected completely – the wage at the end of the week'. Describing the efforts made to provide actual cash-earning experiences for the most unlikely lads in his school, and the effect it had on their attitudes to running their own lives, taking decisions, budgeting, fulfilling obligations, dealing with strangers, as well as such mundane things as using the telephone, Arthur Young remarked:

'We have overcome the ridiculous idea that giving children the chance to earn money in school is somehow immoral ... In the changing situation in ecucation, pupil-teacher relationships and roles are the essence of much heart-searching and debate. We might do well to compare the differences in an earning-learning situation between master and apprentice and in the traditional school situation, captive scholars facing chalk and talk across the barrier of the teacher's desk. The comparison of relationships between newsagent and paperboy and between paperboy and schoolmaster might also be revealing'.[12]

The Terrace and its wardens

The Terrace, in the words of its joint wardens Pat and Dick Kitto, was 'a Victorian house capable of accommodating sixteen children in three dormitories and five or six adults, with a small number of common or activity rooms, and roughly two acres of land'. They saw it not as a school or an annexe to a school but as 'a residential home where a group of adults and children live and learn together'. Visitors were expected to follow the Dartington code of 'useful work' in making their beds and helping on a rota basis in the serving and clearing of meals. The two wardens, it seemed to me at the time, were the ideal couple for their task, with precisely the right, though rare, qualities of integrity, forbearance and sympathy, to make such an experiment work. The reader of Michael Duane's text may wonder what became of them. Today Dick Kitto is a well-known figure in the world of those parents who want to do without schools, and Pat is a familiar figure in Totnes, Devon.

The end of the experiment

The Terrace started slowly and ended abruptly. The 1974 reorganisation of local government put an end to the West Riding education authority, replaced by a new South Yorkshire body with its own priorities. Alec Clegg retired. Royston Lambert left Dartington and the trustees there decided, like the education authority, that 'we can't afford it'. But you have only to read Michael Duane's scrupulous assessment of his observations of The Terrace to be convinced of the need for radical alternatives.

Twenty years later, in a climate of punitive and expensive authoritarianism, with the collapse of the job market for school leavers, John Robinson is resentful and often predatory. We blame him, not the culture that has excluded him. Duane's findings will be important as we stagger into a new century!

Colin Ward

---

1. John R. Dunford, *Central/Local Government Relations 1977-1987 With Special Reference to Education* (Trentham Books for the Association of Education Committees, 1987).

2. Martin Small, 'About Risinghill' in *Anarchy 92*, October 1968, reprinted in *A Decade of Anarchy*, edited by C. Ward (Freedom Press, 1987).

3. Michael Duane, *Work, Language and Education in the Industrial State* (Freedom Press, 1991).

4. Colin Ward, 'The Terrace, Conisbrough' in *BEE – Bulletin of Environmental Education*, No. 27, July 1973.

5. *Children and Their Primary Schools* (HMSO, 1967) – the Plowden Report.

6. A.H. Halsey, Director of the National Educational Priority Area Project in *Educational Priority* (HMSO, 1973).

7. Michael Young, *The Elmhirsts of Dartington: The Creation of an Utopian Community* (Routledge & Kegan Paul, 1982).

8. Royston Lambert, *The Chance of a Lifetime?* (Weidenfeld & Nicolson, 1975).

9. Royston Lambert, *Alternatives to School*, The W.B. Curry Memorial Lecture (University of Exeter, 1972).

10. *Half Our Future* (HMSO, 1963) – the Newsom Report.

11. Alec Clegg, lecture at the Central Hall, Westminster, on the centenary of the 1870 Education Act, printed as 'The Education of John Robinson' in *The Listener*, 13th August 1970.

12. Arthur Young, 'Earning and Learning Your Way Through School', *BEE – Bulletin of Environmental Education*, No. 43, November 1974.

Acknowledgements

I am indebted to numerous friends for many ideas that appear hereafter, especially to Pat Kitto and Dick Kitto and the team whose insights and dedication made the experiment possible.

To Edwin Webb of Garnett College my thanks are due for his perceptive discussions and helpful suggestions for analysing the language used by the students at The Terrace.

I am grateful to the University of Exeter for permission to quote extensively from Royston Lambert's *Alternatives to School*, and to Constable and Co. Ltd. for permission to quote from Carl Rogers' *Child Centred Therapy*.

I am especially indebted to the trustees of Dartington for permission to visit The Terrace over a period of two years.

Throughout I prefer to use 'man' in its original meaning of 'human being' – maintained in dialectical and West Indian usage – rather than the clumsy form 'man/woman' or 'he/she'.

M. Duane

Introduction

The following study was undertaken as part of a larger and continuing study attempting to clarify what we mean by progressive education. It was undertaken because it seemed to offer an opportunity of testing out in practice – in the experimental ROSLA (Raising of the School Leaving Age) scheme set up jointly by Dr Royston Lambert, Head of Dartington Hall School, and Sir Alec Clegg, at that time Director of Education for the West Riding – some of the tentative conclusions being reached in the larger study.

During that study I was having to realise afresh that the focal point of human action was language and the symbolising process in general. All specifically human interaction with others, with himself and with his physical environment are mediated through and depend on the creation and manipulation of symbols; and the range of those symbols extends far beyond those conventionally associated with formal education – words and written symbols – into those necessary for the communication of perceptual experience of all kinds – vocal, aural, visual, proprioceptive and kinaesthetic.

Progressive education, in so far as a unity of definition, purpose and practice can be discerned among its theoreticians and practitioners, by its claim to educate 'the whole man', implies the acquisition of a wider range of linguistic and communicative skills than is normal in schools to which progressive education is held to be an alternative. Further, it claims that learning arising from the child's preoccupations (child-centred) is deeper and more accurate than learning in response to demands made by agencies (teachers, school, examinations) external to the child's original socialisation in the home.

Many years of teaching children in poor areas had caused me to doubt formulations of intelligence that stressed genetic structures, but it was not until the early sixties that I was compelled more closely to re-examine the formulations of Sir Cyril Burt. Perhaps the most obvious stimulus to reconsider my beliefs was provided by A.R. Luria's lectures on *The Role of Speech in the Regulation of Normal and Abnormal Behaviour* and by Dr John Daniels of Nottingham University directing me to some post-war research in this area. This research compelled me to see that the function of language and symbolism was critical both for the individual in becoming fully human and as a means of social cohesion and control. I was then led to read Edward Sapir, Ernst Cassirer, Lev Vygotsky, Suzanne Langer and others, including more recent work by the Gardners on the use of symbols by apes.

The more I read the more it became clear that the concept of intelligence needed re-formulation. I now believe that all human activity other than the type of somatic activity we share with all other vertebrates – eating, breathing, sleeping, etc. – depends on a continuous flow of symbols, external and internal, interacting with sensory experience. Since man has to learn to make, use and interpret symbols in order to communicate (without communication he is not in any normal sense of the word human), 'intelligence' can be more easily understood as efficiency in the use of symbols to solve problems in socially acceptable ways. If this suggestion is correct it makes possible the improvement of intelligence by increasing the range and the level of linguistic skills in the user – 'linguistic', in this context, including all systems of symbols whether aural, as in music; visual, as in painting; kinaesthetic, as in dancing or athletics, and so on.

'The Terrace', as the base for the ROSLA scheme at Conisbrough was known, seemed to be a particularly valuable project for the purpose of this study because the students selected to take part had been chosen as being, in the judgement of the school, more than usually inept intellectually, linguistically and socially. They had been classified as 'non-achievers' or 'drop-outs' because they already had a record of misbehaviour, truancy and general alienation from the purposes of the school such as to cause many of the staff to wish to see them removed from the school as soon as possible.

I was coming to realise that much of progressive education could be seen as a protest against limitations imposed on children's growth by traditional schools and élitist attitudes, and that such protest was part of the much larger and increasing tension between old social habits and beliefs and the emerging needs of an evolving culture.

I was also having to see that whereas language theoretically equips the child to encompass reality in potentially limitless ways, at the same time it actually limits and shapes his perception of that reality to what is acceptable by the group in which he has been reared. In consequence, the problems raised by attempts deliberately to change the goals and forms of education meet with resistance not only at the level of political and social action but within the psychic structures of those who propose and those who oppose change.

Believing that circumstances at The Terrace would favour the growth of linguistic skills, I chose it as a suitable testing ground for the theory, and having learned at about that time that the scheme was likely to run into difficulties and might, indeed, cease for lack of funds, I sought and was granted leave of absence to record discussions at The Terrace during the year 1974-75, as no detailed record of the students' language had been made during the first year of the scheme.

Assumptions made in the study

From what I had seen in private progressive schools, in schools for maladjusted children and in other ROSLA schemes; from what I had learnt from research into learning and from my own experience as a teacher and parent, I made the following assumptions:

a) that self-confidence, as seen in physical bearing, in ease of interaction with others and especially with those recognised to be in authority, would increase as the scheme progressed;

b) that verbal ability, as measured by the range of vocabulary and grammatical structures used or understood, would increase;

c) that bullying, theft, vandalism and insensitivity would diminish;

d) that curiosity about human affairs in general would increase – to the extent that:
(i) the work done was important, satisfying to them or others whom they respected, or was seen to be necessary;
(ii) the control exercised by the adults was accepted as reasonable and democratic, i.e. that the students' views were sought and incorporated in action, or that reasonable grounds were given when not incorporated;
(iii) that the work demanded greater verbal skill than they had previously exercised;
(iv) that the language used by the adults associated with the scheme was seen to be functional and appropriate;

(v) that increased competence in language, skill in work and sensitivity in interaction resulted in more rapid and more accurate communication, drew more approval from others or brought about more effective solutions to the problems on which they were engaged.

Results of the Study

All the assumptions under a), b), c) and d) were borne out by the adults responsible for the running of the scheme, by the parents of the students taking part, by those teachers who continued to meet the students during and after the scheme, by social workers and the Youth Employment Officer who came into contact with them, by employers who assisted with the various projects undertaken by the ROSLA group, by prospective employers who interviewed the students and by the testimony of the students themselves.

Students varied in the degree to which they improved during or as a result of the scheme; some improved in quite remarkable ways while some improved in only one or two areas and so little that it would be unrealistic to claim that the improvement was attributable to the scheme rather than simply to the fact of growing older and gaining more experience. More detailed evidence of progress is presented later.

Again, since no objective assessment of each student's 'starting point' was available, except in terms of school attendance and record of delinquency, little is known about the state of mind or degree of enthusiasm with which they undertook the scheme. Some of the students' own evidence suggests that they were free to opt for the scheme or not as they wished, some suggests that considerable pressure was brought to bear on them to undertake the scheme. From their own evidence some of the students saw the scheme as a chance to develop certain skills that would improve their job prospects; others saw it as a more pleasant form of schooling or as a 'skive'.

Objectives

Since the overall purpose of the study was to test out the idea that an increase in linguistic competence would result in a raising of the level of 'intelligence' or of competence in solving problems, it was obvious that the language used by the students should be studied throughout the experiment for increases in vocabulary and the range of grammatical structures used and/or understood, and related to evidence of greater competence in action or communication.

Further, since language is used in many different contexts which affect the ways in which the speaker will use it, the study should take account of these different contexts and, if possible, of their different psychological and emotional meanings for the speakers. For example, an incident that is seen by a group of students as testing out the sincerity of a teacher will be spoken about in a different manner to that teacher at the time of the incident from the manner used to peers who are also part of the testing-out incident, and again, in a different manner from that used some months after the event to the same teacher when greater confidence in him prevails and to an outside enquirer who is trusted enough to be part of the discussion, even when both the students and the enquirer realise that the discussion may entail criticism of the original teacher or of their own assumptions at the time.

Similarly language will be used to peers in one way when others are not present, but in a different way when there are peers of a different social class present whom the speaker wishes to impress, and in a different way again when the peers to be impressed are from the same background but belong to a different clique or gang. So some account has to be taken of the level of social sensitivity to the language context and of the motives operating in the mind of the speaker. For example, Jack, suddenly thrust into the social, geographical and cultural context of Dartington School very different from his native Conisbrough, indicates his tension and his unease only to his closest friend, but puts on a brave front – a kind of 'hard drinking, hard smoking, silent he-man' pose – for the benefit of the Dartington students, especially the more attractive girls, because that pose both expresses the image that he thinks will impress them and, at the same time, allows him with reason to avoid exposing his most vulnerable area – the use of language according to their style or code. Then again, when he has discovered that some of the Dartington students like him very much, he will change his pose and open out more fully in language to become the 'joker' or the 'life and soul of the party', using his normal speech with more confidence because it interests many of his listeners to the point that *they* start to use it.

Long exposure to the physical and social environment of the school will have established habits of response tested out by the student and accepted as being appropriate. The change to the dramatically different physical environment of The Terrace would itself cause the students to re-assess the validity of their habits and produce a period of uncertainty of response. When further complicated by daily contact as individuals and in small groups with a team of adults who, though clearly in authority, behave in very un-teacherly ways and with very different expectations relating to behaviour, discipline, language, appearance, style of work and achievement, the uncertainty of the students about what is expected of them will be likely to cause them to behave in quite unusual and often bizarre ways. This, in itself, can be seen not as perverse, but as a quite reasonable seeking for norms that will be accepted in the new context.

So adults who seek to make the work and their contacts with the students as reasonable as possible will, for some time, and certainly until they are confident that they have gained some measure of trust from the students, refrain from expressing their opinions of unacceptable behaviour with their normal force and clarity lest they make the establishment of trust more difficult. This, however, may well be viewed by the students as meaning 'anything goes'. Or they may mistake the intentions of the adult, as when Ken's efforts to persuade the boys to resume work after they had declared a 'strike' (because he himself had put so much into the scheme and feared its failure) was seen by the boys as a denial of the previous assurances that it was the boys themselves who would make the important decisions, and as evidence that Ken was simply being 'bossy'.

Methods of Study

1. Gaining familiarity with Conisbrough through meeting people – parents, teachers, employers, doctors, social workers, officials, local councillors and others. Visiting the institutions that form the background of the social life of the area, in particular the Miners Welfare Clubs, the schools, the places of work, so as to understand as much as possible of the social assumptions operating in their daily

life. Many hours were spent in Miners Welfare Clubs, pubs; talking to headmasters, teachers, doctors, social workers and education officials; meeting miners and their wives, mothers and daughters who work regularly in the 'sewing factories', steelmen; retired miners and railmen.

2. Tape-recording the students on the ROSLA scheme in full discussions of the group, as individuals and in small groups; taping groups of their friends not taking part in the scheme; taping groups of boys taking part in a ROSLA scheme based in a church hall but operating on an exam-oriented course.

3. Taping discussions with the adults directly responsible for the ROSLA scheme, and including the school staff co-operating with the ROSLA scheme.

4. Taping discussions with others indirectly concerned with the ROSLA scheme such as Dartington staff and students and parents of Dartington children and others who encountered the Conisbrough students when visiting Dartington.

5. Using diaries, accounts, reports made at the time.

6. In the case of the 1973-74 group, taping a discussion with as many members of that group as could be found, taping discussions with the adults who took part in that scheme, and using the diaries and reports made during that year.

7. Observing the speech and behaviour of members of the 1973-74 group when they spent two and a half hours discussing their work with experienced teachers taking an Advanced Diploma in the University of Nottingham. Observing the 1973-74 group when they spent several days visiting London. Speaking to Neal and Pat on that occasion.

8. Listening to the reactions of those people who visited The Terrace between 1973 and 1975.

9. Studying evaluations by the students and by others directly and indirectly concerned with the ROSLA schemes.

Notes
Unfortunately the headmaster would not allow standardised tests of any kind to be administered to the students, so comparisons of 'intelligence' or of levels of English and mathematics at the beginning of the experiment with those at the end could not be made. Reports by experienced teachers who had taught the students before the experiment could not be matched with reports by the same teachers afterwards since the students were not again taught by these teachers.

Reports by teachers, employers and social workers familiar with similar students from Northcliffe School and other schools of that type might seem to be useful indicators, but have dubious value because the content and form of such reports depend on so many variables, such as whether the reporter is sympathetic or not the student reported on; whether he understands or approves of the purposes for which the report is being made; to what extent there is confidence or rapport between the reporter and the one requesting the report; his state of mood at the time of making the report ...

One has only to have had experience as head of a school to see how the same teacher will make quite substantial changes in the character and tone of reports about the same pupil according to the changes in his relationships with the pupil, according to his relationships with the parents and according to his relationships with his head of department or head of school who will also read the reports.

Part I
Origins of the Conisbrough Experiment

In his W.B. Curry Memorial Lecture at the University of Exeter, *Alternatives to School*, delivered on 19th November 1971, Dr Royston Lambert, appointed some two years previously as Head of Dartington Hall School, asked the question '*Has* the progressive ethic in education got a future? In particular, have the independent radical schools ... any further creative role to play in the development of national patterns of education? Or have they gone the way of all institutions devoted to expressive ideals, like the Church, frozen into the archaic orthodoxy of the minority, ceased to develop internally or to relate externally, become isolated rural communities pursuing aims which the countless visitors who flock to them usually admire, and on leaving promptly forget?'

He defined the 'progressive ethic' in these terms:

'1. First the child is seen as a distinct individual whose *whole* development is the concern of education: personal, creative, social, moral and emotional growth being viewed as important as the development of basic skills.
2. Second, as people differ so their patterns of development may differ and thus individuals are allowed to develop at their own pace, supported by structures or stimulated by pressures which apply to that individual alone. They are not judged by collective standards and attributes or fashioned to an ideal model type of person.
3. It follows thirdly that children as individual moral beings are encouraged to acquire their own values in an open society and not have certain selected values thrust upon them in the process of growth.
4. Equally, as moral agents, children are allowed to decide for themselves on all matters of personal taste and expression, and when the exercise of such freedom clashes with that of others, they are subject to processes of democratic decision: likewise when matters affecting their own long or short term interests are at stake, they have a real share in the making of decisions.
5. As everyone is either personally free or bound by decisions in which they genuinely participate, control is therefore a matter of self-discipline; there is no need for external rewards or sanctions or hierarchies or systems of authority and promotion.

6. As young people are moral agents, they are equal to older ones who are the same: older people have experience which may deserve respect (it all depends on what the experience is and what they have made of it), young people have a lack of experience which definitely commands respect. Therefore relations between young and adult in education should be warm and informal, not based on fear or false ideas of authority. These in abstract terms are the basic components of the progressive ethic.'

The acceptance of the progressive ethic had followed quite naturally in the primary schools because it accorded with new thinking in psychology and because, in addition, 'very young children can only expect to play a limited part in decision making, and therefore the problem of participation in democracy is avoided'. Secondary schools had not been seriously affected by the progressive ethic because examination and preparation for careers added to the unresolved role conflicts of adult and adolescent. Even within the original group of progressive schools only Kilquhanity, Monkton Wyld, St Christopher's, Wenington, Summerhill and Dartington had maintained 'the full, unadulterated ethic'. Attempts such as Risinghill and Braehead, to apply progressive ideals within state secondary schools, had failed. It remained to be seen whether Countesthorpe would survive.

Dr Lambert then questioned the role of the progressive schools as explorers. What was to be their role if Countesthorpe should succeed? What had Dartington itself done in the previous three years as evidence that it was rethinking its role? Critics had alleged that progressive schools emphasised expressive rather than instrumental powers after selecting children of progressive parents, and they questioned how effective the progressives would be with working-class children.

'To meet this criticism, and because a one class residential ghetto is scarcely an enriching educational experience anyway, Dartington had redeployed its endowment and linked up with one of the most deprived and totally working-class educational priority areas in the country and has similarly linked with the two vocational training units for young boys on the Dartington estate. In all in the last two years about sixty young people over the age of 15, all eleven-plus failures, all fashioned in secondary modern schools and working-class housing estates and not specially selected, have become full-time residents at a school with a total of 200 boarding places. Over 400 other children from the EPA in the North have also lived and worked at the school on short-term educational courses ... One can say already and with confidence that the progressive educational approach applies as much to the working-class adolescent and to the less able child as to those pre-socialised and highly able. Signals from Countesthorpe indicate that they are experiencing the same thing.'

Critics also alleged that the progressives were closed in values, conformist and isolated, and no realistic preparation for ordinary life. This was largely true, but Dartington had shown that the school could respond to a heterogeneous culture with competing and conflicting styles. Further, it was trying to make its students more closely aware of the world in which they lived.

'... some children do full-time paid jobs or apprenticeships and still live in the school (we even have one on national assistance), some work regularly in the undertakings owned by the Trust as part of their course. 135 pupils have lived and studied at our sister school in Yorkshire, where there are over 1,000 children. Our social work ranges from our base in Sicily where students live for a year or more among grinding peasant poverty and the mafia, to the Yorkshire coalfield where we have another base amid mass unemployment and poor housing. No-one could pass through the school without direct personal experience of a wide range of social, industrial and moral circumstances.'

(Note: reasons for ceasing to send Dartington children to study in Northcliffe School – the poor quality of the teaching and the lack of personal attention. M.D.)

But even the most radical schools had made the same assumptions about education:

1. They segregated children from life.

2. They put them in specially designed and equipped premises with specially trained adults.

3. They controlled their time, social grouping and activities for externally imposed purposes.

4. They created a curriculum.

In fact they were doing what was done to every child in Western society. Everyone sought to make the process more effective. None questioned whether it was all worth the effort or what the point was. The de-schoolers did question what school was for, but some of their assertions – such as that all institutions were degrading or dehumanising – were questionable. But we could not deny that for large numbers school was ineffective. We had therefore to look for alternatives if only for them.

'This experiment [Conisbrough] is based on no general political doctrines ... it does not derive from dogma at the macrocosmic level but from pragmatic observation of the actual needs of children over some years, and in particular of the working-class adolescents who will form this kind of group.'

He then outlined ten principles for the running of such an experiment:

1. Continuous and sympathetic support by adults other than parents.

2. A base other than the home near the centre of the town, with beds, private space, workshop space, recreational space.

3. Co-operative work with adults as well as peers.

4. Real decision making about work, money earned, etc.

5. Activity to be continuous and organic rather than broken up into regular intervals irrespective of the work in hand.

6. A float of money; care of the base and the organisation and preparation of communal meals; economic ventures such as part-time jobs ... to be used as the raw material for the real-life decisions that make for growth of personality, values and skills.

Unpaid social service to be encouraged and as much time to be devoted to it as required. Cultural activity of three kinds:
i) individual and group creative work of all kinds;
ii) exploration of local culture – trade unions, working men's clubs, commercial culture, religious group culture;
iii) more general culture such as art galleries, country houses, concerts, museums.

From all this experience to explore central issues that arise – personal relations and sex, ethical problems, spiritual and religious problems, economic especially unemployment problems, problems of violence, politics, scientific and technological issues.

7. A wide range of facilities with the school as a resource centre, e.g. libraries, factories, voluntary organisations, men's clubs.

8. All members to remain in the group if they wish even when they are legally entitled to take up work after reaching the leaving age.

9. The group to plan its own expeditions, physical activities and use of local and other clubs and facilities. Dartington and its resources to be available to the group for such purposes.

10. The LEA to provide a sum equalling the per capita cost of each pupil as if he was in full-time schooling.

This was only one of the many possible alternatives to schooling. The deliberate disintegration of the school which has happened at Dartington into a cluster of inter-related units of varying scale, structure and independence, showed possible bridges between school and more informal related bases and groups. Vocational units, day and residential, offered enormous scope for development as alternatives to schooling. The school's own social work base in Sicily offered an education in itself, since the young people had to learn a language, to know the social and artistic history of Mediterranean Europe and the sociology of peasant societies, to have basic skills in accounting, cookery, driving, farming and child care, and special skills ranging from teaching to pottery and agriculture. Schools themselves might take in ex-pupils who had become young wage earners and apprentices and give them support, ending that most soulless of all institutional processes, the day-release scheme. Such development would threaten many vested interests, the structure of teaching pay, trade unions and examination bodies.

'When I came to Dartington in January 1969 I wrote in an article in *New Society* that I hoped 'to become non-head of an anti-school, the first of many'. No-one understood what I meant at the time and the phrase has been much ridiculed ever since. Perhaps its meaning is now more clear. For those who adopt the radical stance to education the ideal flexible and educational setting to which one looks is not Summerhill or Countesthorpe but possibly that centre put up by the boys, fathers and elders of the Vai Tribe in West Africa. Together they build a structure to suit their needs, numbers and activities.

When the group's training is over, by way of celebrating their arrival at manhood, they burn the structure to the ground. It is an end of term ceremony which every English schoolboy would be eager to emulate. It is one which much of the structure of present schooling deserves. And it displays an attitude of mind which, if education is to match the needs of children and their society, all of us would do well to adopt.'

Part II
ROSLA I (1973-74): the First Term

During the summer of 1973 plans were completed for the first experimental ROSLA scheme to start at The Terrace in the following September. Talks were held with the head of Northcliffe School to clarify the principles on which the scheme should run. He had already had a copy of Royston Lambert's lecture at Exeter University and had raised no objections to any of the principles outlined at that time, or to the more detailed application set out in his paper *Alternative to School* published and circulated to the staffs of both Dartington Hall and Northcliffe Schools during the summer of 1971.

It was agreed that fifteen boys should be given the opportunity to take part in the scheme, boys for whom the staff had no academic ambitions even at the level of CSE, or who themselves had shown no interest in academic work. The two wardens, Pat and Dick Kitto, were, for the first few weeks at least, to be relieved of their responsibility for organising and running courses for the groups of Dartington pupils staying at The Terrace. These courses were suspended for that time so that the wardens could assist with the ROSLA scheme on a full-time basis to give it the best possible start.

In addition to the two wardens one young full-time teacher, Neal, was appointed by Northcliffe, and one young man, not trained as a teacher but having extensive experience of youth work, Ken, was appointed by Dartington. The local authority made a house available at Conisbrough for Ken and his family. Neal had been born and bred in Conisbrough and was thoroughly familiar not only with the boys and their parents but also with many of the local employers and officials, a fact that was to be important in finding paid work for the boys to do as part of the scheme.

Responsibility for the conduct of the scheme was to rest with the head of Northcliffe and to be exercised from day to day through Neal. Later discussions with the wardens, particularly during ROSLA II, the second scheme in 1974-75, indicate that the location and precise responsibility for the scheme had not been so clearly set out and understood as was believed. Confusion about final responsibility was to grow in ROSLA II as it began to be realised that the head's understanding of the implications of the 'Dartington ethos' was not what had been imagined in the early months. Originally Royston Lambert had proposed living part-time in Conisbrough and being responsible for the scheme.

Further, the original plan envisaged a close interaction between the school and The Terrace by enabling the ROSLA students to attend school for whatever lessons they chose, but as time went by the boys preferred to remain at The Terrace for the whole of their time. Many chose to do this because the meals prepared at The Terrace were to them much more palatable than school meals. Part of the reason for their not visiting the school during the first term was to avoid contact with the many staff who had been critical of them while they were at school, though this changed later in the year.

On Monday 3rd September 1973, the first group of boys arrived at The Terrace. It was clear that they had been chosen for the scheme
a) because they wanted to leave school at the first opportunity;
b) because they had no interest in academic work and were considered incapable of sitting for even the CSE examination;
c) that many of them had been in trouble with the police;
d) that nearly all of them were regarded by the school staff as disruptive nuisances;
e) that they all had very poor records of attendance at school, with an average absence rate of over 40%.

From what I was able to observe of the boys during the early weeks of the scheme it was clear that they would have been classified by many traditional teachers as 'loutish' in behaviour. They smoked openly and with an air of defiance; during meetings with the staff they lounged in a way that seemed to invite the staff to rebuke them; they were slow to start any work and had to be constantly urged to get on with it; they arrived late and without apology or explanation; they left early if they could do so, and without clearing up or tidying away tools and materials; in discussions about their work or plans for work and outings they left decisions to the staff and were extremely reluctant to commit themselves to an opinion. The general air of slovenliness and of contemptuous indifference to the views and wishes of adults, together with an undercurrent of sly vulgarity, seemed intended to force the adults into behaving as many of their teachers had behaved towards them in school. And as the adults continued to use reason and patience they seemed to be resentful that they were *not* responding as their teachers had done.

However, by the third week their attitudes had begun to change. The staff had worked closely with the boys and had encouraged them cheerfully by example. They had taken them out to an art exhibition in Sheffield; had visited the Doncaster Races and interviewed punters and others with a tape-recorder; had visited Matlock and done some climbing with Ken; had started to rehearse a Mummers Play, and had done work that was highly commended by a local builder and decorator. The diary written by Neal gives a day by day account of their work and discussions and of their responses to the changed conditions.

From the beginning the adults sought to deal with problems of discipline by raising them as matters of concern in the meetings. At first the boys were reluctant to voice their opinions, as they found discussions boring and preferred to 'get on with the jobs in the morning and leave the discussion to the adults'. Even though they took every occasion to stop work or to 'muck about', they very much preferred the practical activities of gardening, decorating or repairing the greenhouse to sitting down and thinking out the work to be done or examining the misdemeanours of members of the group.

During the first week attendance was 92%. During the second week it dropped to 77%. In the third week it rose to 98%. It was during the third week that the builder and decorator had commended their work and given his opinion that it should be paid at the full adult rate. Thereafter the attendance of the group never fell below 92% for the remainder of that fourteen week term. An analysis of their activities during this first term shows three broad areas – daily work within or associated with The Terrace; activities, visits, work and contact with other institutions and people; and the control of the group and its affairs.

Work

a) Paid work undertaken by the group for the purpose of financing its

other activities was as follows:
- Interior decoration of The Terrace under the technical guidance of a local builder and decorator.
- Conversion of the Coach House into a workshop – concreting the floor and making workbenches.
- Work on an allotment growing vegetables.
- Repairing a shed for use as a henhouse and keeping poultry.
- Potato picking on local farms.
- Repairing furniture; buying old furniture, cannibalising it and re-selling.
- Reconditioning trolleys for a local firm.
- Repairing hutches and keeping rabbits.
- Making a dog kennel.
- Making jigsaw puzzles.

Note: Paid work for the decoration and repair of The Terrace was coming to an end by the end of the first term. This was the first sign that Dartington was going to reduce its financial commitment to the ROSLA scheme.

b) Unpaid work undertaken by the group to help maintain The Terrace and the grounds surrounding it:
- Clearing the grounds of The Terrace of rubbish.
- Weeding the garden.
- Tidying up the yard.
- Repairing the steps at the entrance to The Terrace.
- Repairs to the minibus trailer.
- Repairing a large store cupboard for the workshop.
- Cleaning and polishing floors.
- Cleaning the minibus.
- Fitting stove in rest room.
- Lighting the fire in their rest room.
- Preparing tea, washing up and collecting money.
- Making a coat rack for the group.

Other activities

a) Work or activities, with other associations or individuals, or new activities for the enlargement of the group's experience and for their greater understanding of local and national structures and events:

- Special lessons at Northcliffe, as chosen by the group, mainly for games and practical lessons in the workshops. These did not last long.
- Writing to the local council for approval to erect a henhouse.
- Visit to the Edvard Munch Exhibition in Sheffield.
- Seeking advice from neighbouring allotment holders about how to run an allotment, deal with 'club root', etc.
- Visiting Doncaster races and tape-recording punters and others.
- Attending courses at Dartington on metalwork, welding, etc.
- Preparing a social evening for their parents and friends.
- Climbing in Derbyshire and touring Matlock.
- Sketching on the moors.
- Visit to Chatsworth House.
- Camping tour of the Dales and camping in Wales.
- Camping tour of the Dales with group of Dartington sixth formers.
- Discussion with visiting MP about the Education (Work Experience) Bill.
- Similar discussions with the YEO.
- helping to prepare the hall for the Careers Convention at Doncaster.
- Visit to Grimsby Docks and Fish Market.
- Visit to Brigg Cattle Market.
- Working with a local garage as part of work experience.
- Discussion with fishermen about the first Cod War.
- Visit to a long-distance trawler.
- Instruction in dancing for the Mummers Play.
- Visit to Magistrate's Court for trial of a brother of one of the group.
- Meeting with Tony Christie, a pop star and brother of Neal.

- Listening to jazz, pop and classical records.
- Map reading and First Aid for camping and climbing.
- Interview on Sheffield Radio.
- Visit to the Crucible Theatre, Sheffield, to see *Uncle Vanya*.
- Visit to Sheffield to see *A Day in the Life of Ivan Denisovich*.
- Visit to the Army Camp at Strensall.
- Visit to Cadeby Pit.
- Visit to a steelworks.
- Attending a course in photography.
- Visit to St Catherine's Hospital for the Severely Subnormal (see note).
- Visit to Bretton Hall College of Education for fishing, sailing and canoeing.
- Chopping logs and sticks for local OAPs.
- Visit to the Ice Rink at Sheffield.
- Work for the Old People's Community Centre.
- Readings by Dick to the group.
- Visit to Beaford, local industries, schools, etc.

Note: some boys were reluctant to visit St Catherine's Hospital. There is a strong local prejudice against, and fear of, people who are mentally handicapped. On the way to the hospital the boys were obviously very anxious. They were taken round by the matron who carefully explained, as far as she could, how the individual patients were handicapped and how they were treated to try and improve their competence. On the way back the boys were deeply concerned and moved by the difficulties of the patients and asked whether they could do regular work in the hospital. This was later arranged.

b) **Work undertaken to improve their ability to express themselves orally and in writing:**

- Mummers Play.
- Writing up of diaries of work done and places visited.
- Attachment to the Foxfire Course – a joint study of the local neighbourhood by members of the group together with students from Dartington.

- Daily meetings of the group to discuss work, deal with misdemeanours, make decisions about the running of the group, visits, etc. In these meetings discussion and responsibility was, as far as possible, made to rest with the members of the group.
- Inviting friends to lunch at The Terrace.
- Preparing of agenda for meetings and charts of events for the term.
- Joining in the Dartington Sixth Form Course run at The Terrace.
- Taking meals with the Dartington Sixth Form Course.
- Individual tuition in reading and writing at boys' request.
- Joining the Edward VI School course.
- A series of lunchtime discussions with outside speakers on topics such as Catholicism, Hinduism, politics, birth control, abortion, and other current issues.
- Discussions with the many visitors to The Terrace.

The control of the group and its affairs

During the first few weeks the group was reluctant to talk or to indicate that they were willing to co-operate. Everything was done by the boys to make it appear that they were being pushed unwillingly into the activities of The Terrace. They required encouragement to work consistently, to tidy up, to arrive on time and not to leave early.

'It was clear from later discussion with the staff that many of the suggestions coming out at the meetings were from the adults because at this time the boys were so clearly reluctant to speak in a group. Much of their behaviour in the groups showed how uneasy they were. They slouched into the armchairs as if to avoid notice; they smoked; they answered in monosyllables; they sniggered frequently and made *sotto voce* comments to one another. Their general behaviour and demeanour was that of young people thoroughly alienated not only from school but from adults in any position of what they regarded as "authority".' (Diary of the First Term)

It was in the second week that the first discussion about behaviour in the group took place.

'Two boys had been bullying Steven to the point where he asked to leave the ROSLA group and return to school. We consoled him and promised to deal with the offenders the following morning. Next morning the two miscreants were informed of the consequences of their actions; they were very surprised that he was so hurt and said they did not realise he was so easily offended. We pointed out that in a small group such as ours it was essential to be sensitive towards other members in order to avoid the friction caused by close working conditions. Finally it was pointed out that Steven had no father and was probably more likely to be upset by such actions. The boys were apologetic and rather sheepish.' (Diary)

At the same meeting complaints were made by the staff about litter and debris left uncleared and about members of the group who could not be left to work unsupervised. At this meeting Neil undertook to read minutes of the previous meeting.

During this week the group was offered various courses at Dartington but it was clear that the prospect of staying away from home was too strange for them. The staff persisted and, in smaller groups, finally persuaded some boys to undertake some courses. Later, of course, it was found that they enjoyed the courses very much and there was no more reluctance.

In the third week the adults complained of slackness and unpunctuality and demanded notes for absence. It was clear that the group did not like either the complaints about their behaviour or the demand that they share in the discussions. Later in this week the local builder came to assess their work in decoration:

'He was quite taken aback by the standard of the work done, saying it was 'really excellent', 'out of this world' and a credit to their efforts. He costed the job at £66.89 (£26.74 for the small downstairs room and £40.15 for the dormitory). The only criticisms were that they had used too much paint (twice that required for the job) and had not taken enough care with the wiping-up of spots on the floors. He finished by saying that the work done was equal to that done by his employees but that the boys had taken a good deal longer in the execution of the work.' (Diary)

This was clearly an important turning-point in their feelings about themselves. Attendance for that week rose to 98%.

Towards the end of the fourth week some of the boys complained that they were kept waiting while the staff had their staff meetings first thing in the morning; there were complaints about Alex using his job as storeman to avoid 'real work'. These were some of the first indications that they were entering into the spirit of the ROSLA scheme and accepting the fact that they too had some share in decisions.

It was in the fifth week that the first meeting took place in which the staff played little part. For four weeks the group had been working in The Terrace, had made a number of visits to the Dales and elsewhere, had begun rehearsals for the Mummers Play, and had had complaints about behaviour, untidiness and so on, but had experienced no punishment. Reasons had always been given for the demands made of them. Each day, so far as possible, had begun afresh in terms of relationships. It had begun to be obvious that the staff were always available, and were prepared to work with the boys in the evenings if they wished.

The meeting started with discussion of points written on the agenda – a disco evening, change of rehearsal times and the slashing of James' bicycle tyre the day before. This resulted in heated argument that extended the meeting for well over an hour. Paul suggested that the group pay James some restitution; Alex refused to contribute his 1p and was then outlawed or 'sent to Coventry' by the rest.

'This was by far the best meeting to date and everyone contributed in some way to the argument. For the first time the staff took a back seat while the boys conducted the argument; group sensitivity and group awareness seemed to be developing.' (Diary)

Later in the day someone let down the tyres on Alex's bicycle, as if to punish him further for his refusal to contribute to the cost of repairing James' tyre.

The staff were not always agreed about how to deal with, for example, idleness. For the trip to Grimsby Pat had allowed some boys to sleep at The Terrace so that they could make an early start. Neal was to pick the others up on the way, going, if necessary, to the homes of those who had overslept. Ken argued that such laxity should be punished simply by not taking them on the trip. Neal argued in reply that the boys were at a stage when they had to be encouraged to undertake new experiences.

At the end of that week only Neal happened to be free to chair the weekly meeting of the group:

'From the outset the boys seemed reluctant to speak and Neal asked them why this was so. They replied that they still considered him 'a teacher' because they did not feel able to swear in his company. Neal said that he thought swearing to be lazy, unnecessary and restrictive of their ability to express themselves. The boys countered by saying that Dick and Ken swore occasionally in front of them and that it seemed more natural for them to do so. Neal pointed out that Dick and Ken could express themselves extremely well without swearing and that he thought it important for the boys to develop this ability first rather than lapse into poor expression by laziness and lack of practice of more formal speech. He said that if anyone found real difficulty in speaking without swearing then he would rather they swore.' (Diary)

Two weeks later Neil complained that Neal had added an item to the agenda on his behalf without consulting him. The group decided to appoint a chairman from among themselves. Later in that same week they decided to change rehearsal timings and times for working on the diaries. Steven asked for additional rehearsals as time was running short. They agreed. It was beginning to be accepted that they had the power to arrange the details of the course to suit their own wishes and they were acting on this.

In the ninth week the staff, who had been feeling worried about Paul's relative isolation from the group, agreed that Neal and Ken should have a talk with him. When they did so Paul admitted that he did not get on well with the rest of the group and promised to try and improve in this and in his general attitude to work. During the next two weeks he was obviously trying hard. Then there occurred an incident that seemed to indicate a change of attitude towards him by the group:

'While the group was waiting for the afternoon meeting to begin the phone rang. Paul, who was nearest, refused to answer it. He then admitted that he was nervous at the thought. The boys reacted in a concerned manner – which they usually did not do with Paul – and encouraged him instead or deriding him. This reaction seemed to stem from his obvious attempts to get on better with the group.' (Diary)

During one meeting at this time, soon after the half-term break, a discussion arose about relationships in the group and at The Terrace. Neal had suggested that there was less bullying at The Terrace than at school and less violence in general. Ken agreed and asked why this should be so. Peter thought it was because bullying could be more easily spotted at The Terrace than at school because there was closer supervision. Neil thought that it was because he had changed in himself and felt less like bullying others. It was at this time that the head of Northcliffe visited The Terrace and commented very favourably on the quality of the boys' work and on their mature and confident manner.

During this second half of the term it was noticeable that the boys spent longer at The Terrace, working in the workshop or completing something they had begun, rather than rushing home as soon as the time came. Paul worked until 6pm on several occasions – 'Because I want to get it finished', and others spent much of their Saturdays and Sundays on the allotment or in the workshop. After one weekend building a chicken shed, a dog kennel, a workbench and two rabbit hutches with John Shirtcliffe, a local steel worker who worked with and advised the boys on their woodwork, Paul said, 'I wish we could do this every weekend. I'd be only sat in the house doing nothing or hanging about the streets. It'd keep me out of trouble.'

When the boys visited Strensall Army Camp and went through an assault course they were pitted against three groups from schools in Doncaster and Barnsley. The Terrace group came top in the result and it was noticed that the stronger members deliberately refrained from finishing first themselves in order to help the weaker members over the more difficult obstacles.

In the week that he returned from a Dartington course Peter, who had had a talk from Neal about his general attitude and performance at The Terrace, was enthusiastic about the course and almost completely transformed in his attitude to the group and to the ROSLA scheme in general, and was instrumental in helping others to see the course in a more favourable light.

It began to be seen that they were becoming more interested in the world outside The Terrace and Conisbrough.

'After lunch the group sat around in the quiet room talking and playing cards. The staff began to talk among themselves about the Watergate affair. Dave Hatton listened with interest and then asked various questions which the staff answered. "I'm interested in things like that. I'm gonna have to start reading the newspapers and watching the news".

Neal asked if they were interested in having a discussion one lunchtime each week on some current topic such as the Middle East war or the fuel crisis. Dave agreed and various others chipped in from time to time from their card-playing to say they were interested. The current affairs discussions were arranged for Tuesday lunchtimes.'

The first discussion was then arranged and was on Northern Ireland.

When Neal arranged for the group to play the school Paul refused to play for The Terrace, claiming that he was a member of the school team. The others were quite angry with him:

Peter: I think you should have some loyalty for the group and stuff the school team.

Paul: Stuff The Terrace team! I want to continue playing for them [the school]. I've not missed a match and I'm not starting now.

At which the others called him 'traitor', 'swine' and so on, but Paul stuck to his decision.

During this discussion, when Neal had suggested arranging a series of games with other teams or joining a league, most agreed but Alex said 'Wait and see what we're like before you make any fixtures' – a feeling with which the others then agreed and indicated a new-found caution that had not been seen before in discussions about their own powers as players. Later in the same meeting when they were discussing the Duke of Edinburgh's Award Scheme, Ken and some of the group said that the scheme was a kind of 'carrot' which distracted from the intrinsic pleasure or benefit of the particular activity:

Peter: I just want to climb the fourteen peaks in Snowdonia. I don't want a certificate to prove I've done it; I just want to do it so I'll know I can do it.

Steven: But if you did the fourteen peaks and they offered you a certificate would you take it?

Peter (after a pause): No.

Steven: Look, if something's going and it's a qualification you take it. It doesn't mean you don't enjoy the activity.

ROSLA I (1973-74): the first term

Peter: I just want to climb the fourteen peaks.

The argument continued long after the normal end of the day.

On the Friday of the twelfth week the group performed their Mummers Play for the first time to the Dartingtonians who were about to leave after finishing the Foxfire course. Although it had been clear during the course that the Dartingtonians had done the best work in writing and that the ROSLA group had produced poor work although they had worked very hard, nevertheless the groups seemed to get on well together. The ROSLA group were extremely shy about performing the play but they did so and then escorted the Dartingtonians to the station to see them off. On their return they were unusually quiet and subdued for the rest of the day. During the afternoon they met with Ken for the start of a course of instruction in first aid and map reading. Ian began the meeting by saying:

Ian: I've learned five big words since those Dartos were here.

James: 'Moron' sounds better than 'idiot'.

Dave: What about 'cretin'.

And they go so excited displaying their new words and were so full of compliments for the 'Dartos' that Ken had to call the meeting to order.

Later Neal suggested that those who were entitled to leave at Easter should stay for the full year in order to benefit more fully. Several said they would stay if they could not get jobs. Others asked if they could come back if they did not like their jobs and were told they could. They also asked whether they could come back at weekends or on their rest days and were told that they could.

On the Monday morning of the thirteenth week Neal was met by Peter who had been thrown out by his father on the Saturday night after an argument. He had spent the weekend with his grandmother:

Peter: My dad had something to drink and started arguing with my sisters. I told them they were all acting like children. My dad clouted me so I clouted him back and he threw me out.

Neal: Had you had anything to drink?

Peter: Only four or five pints.

Later that morning Neal visited Peter's father who said that Peter would have to curb his drinking and arguing. He agreed to have him back in the house.

On the Tuesday Neal and Ken gave Peter the 'private talk' that the staff had some time before agreed that Peter required by reason of his aggressive behaviour and his unpopularity with the group. When they told him he was lazy, gluttonous, aggressive and unpopular, Peter shouted: "Well, if you think that of me I'll leave and go back to school!" They pointed out that that was the opinion not only of the staff but of the boys and gave examples to support their case. Peter burst into tears and left The Terrace. Later in the day, on his way to the school, Neal noticed Peter sitting in the small park near the church and beckoned him. Peter came to the car and then sat until Neal had finished his business at the school. Neal told him that Pat and Dick had agreed that he could come down and stay at The Terrace if he thought that it might avoid a fight with his father at any time. Peter thanked him but thought that it would be alright. He went back with Neal and worked alone for the rest of the day.

That same afternoon, when Alan was being criticised for slackness about his weekly duties, he started to get angry, but when he saw that the group as a whole agreed with the criticism he accepted the rebuke and smiled.

Two days later the group was to perform their play to parents and other guests at The Terrace. They had a severe attack of nerves and wanted to call the whole thing off. In fact the play was the great event of the evening. The boys performed with gusto and aplomb. Later they acted as hosts to their guests in showing them around.

Dave: Who was that bloke with the cigar?

Neal: 'Pom' Elmhurst, one of the trustees at Dartington.

Dave: 'E was alright. He didn't just walk in and say everything was great; he tested things like the chicken shed, shook them to see if they was strong and then said what he thought. More honest, I think.

Paul: I thought that. Too many people walk in and say 'Great' without really looking. He took his time and did it right.

The appreciation of the visitors and of the parents for their performance really took the boys by surprise. Peter asked whether he could make his part in the play bigger. They displayed a level of excitement about the work of The Terrace as if they had suddenly realised that they were the centre of attention in Conisbrough – which at this time they were. They began to be noticeably more careful about their personal appearance and to think and behave with more care. At a meeting where some of the group had asked whether they could bring friends to work in the workshop of an evening Dave and James were unwilling:

Dave: They won't care about the place!

Ian: My mates would!

James: There'll be vandalism, I can tell you. They'll break tools through not using them properly.

Finally they voted *not* to bring their friends to the workshop in the evenings.

In the following week they performed their play as part of the Christmas Festival at the school. It was recognised by everyone as a great success. Later in the week they performed it several times for each of the local junior schools, persuading the children to join them in the dancing. At one school they were very critical of the fact that the discipline of the school seemed to be very strict:

Dave: Did you see how they were marched out like machines?

Paul: They were sat there like dummies – daren't move. They couldn't join in like at Morley Place and Station Road.

Steve: The paintings were great on the walls though!

At one school the deputy headmistress booked them to perform to the school for the following Christmas.

During this week Paul had had to appear in court for his part in a break-in at a local woodworking factory. He was fined £5.55. When he returned to The Terrace someone said, 'It's time you behaved yourself!' Paul replied, 'It happened before I joined the group. I wouldn't do it now.' Then the group discussed whether they should help to pay Paul's fine, but decided that such help would be tantamount to a licence to commit crime.

During this week the Youth Employment Officer came to interview them about possible jobs. Afterwards he spoke to the staff and expressed himself as very much impressed by their ability to express themselves – 'far better than their peers at school'. He was also surprised that their attitudes were so thoughtful and mature – 'they obviously have their feet on the ground and are not aiming at jobs far above their capabilities'.

On the Thursday they had arranged a party but only Paul had brought a girlfriend. The others were so nervous at the responsibility of running the party – in spite of plenty of good food prepared by Pat and the cooks – that they stood around in almost total silence until 10pm when they went home.

The staff thought that The Terrace should be used by more pupils from the junior schools in the evenings, and especially the workshop. After several had disagreed they decided to allow the juniors to use it provided they themselves supervised it at these times.

The rest of the diary is a similar record of the activities of the group and of their growth into new forms of self-discipline and awareness.

Part III
ROSLA I (1973-74): Dialogue with Dave

In this section there follow extracts from dialogues with Dave. Other people present on each occasion have been noted at the head of each extract.

In reading these transcriptions it is important to bear in mind

a) that all of these boys were talking *after* their year's experience on the ROSLA scheme at The Terrace. They had all left school; they were all members of 'the world outside school'. Where dialogues with the ROSLA II pupils reveal attitudes in the making, these discussions with the first group of boys tend to reveal completed attitude changes;

b) that they are speaking to or in the presence of people who are closely familiar with The Terrace, the staff (Pat and Dick) and the boys themselves, or with people deeply sympathetic to the purposes of the scheme (Pat Downing and M. Duane).

In all these excerpts the lads make quite explicit what the ROSLA scheme meant to them – *on reflection*. They are also aware, in everything they say, that the listeners are familiar with the detailed history of the scheme: they can, therefore, assume large areas of tacit understanding. For example, in Excerpt B (page 52, line 3 onwards), when in the phrase 'wi them Starcross girls coming up' Dave refers to an event that had precipitated action leading to a critical reappraisal by the boys of their own part in the scheme. That Dave was right in assuming that everyone knew what he was referring to and that, therefore, he had no need to 'spell it out', was confirmed by the slight nods of those listening to him.

It is also important to remember that, to some extent, the lads were aware, during their time at The Terrace, that they were 'pioneers': they were the first group to undertake this scheme. They sensed, therefore, that they were not merely passively 'receiving' a course, but that they were actively constructing that course for themselves, in consultation with others. This new sense of responsibility had to 'grow' in them: whereas their new-found 'freedom' was immediately apparent, the necessary obligations which that imposed had to be learned.

Perhaps this sense of maturity is the most important of all the self-recognitions made by the boys. Certainly they themselves, as they now see themselves, judge themselves as they were. These, their own judgements, are the most important testimonies to that sense of self-development and achievement.

Dialogue I – Dave

When ROSLA I started in September 1973 Dave was fifteen. He was tall, somewhat lanky, with a pale skin, fair reddish hair and a gentle and pleasing expression with good-looking features. Physically he was stronger and tougher than he appeared and could hold his own with his more obviously robust friends, Neil ('Nelly') and Ian.

He spoke with a rather slow drawl, was slow to offer an opinion, but when animated could speak with vigour and make his point forcefully.

He did not put himself out to please or curry favour: in fact he was identified, during the early days of the scheme, with the less co-operative group. When he had made up his mind about a situation or about people he made his own position clear and was a determined opponent or a very loyal friend. When he wanted to he worked hard, long and well.

In the group he was a close friend of the leaders Neil and Ian, though not himself regarded as a leader by the rest of the group. His opinion was valued by the others and, later, by the staff.

Dave suffered from periods of deep depression, especially when frustrated over things he considered important. He found it difficult to control those moods. It was reported that his mother had been in hospital for depression on one occasion. He had a deep affection for her and, as the scheme drew to an end, was torn between a desire to get away from home and a desire to stay to 'protect' his mother.

He seemed to find it difficult to make relations with girls but as he came to know Ken became friendly with both Ken and Angela, Ken's wife, and would visit them and spend whole evenings talking with them; they respected his intelligence and his willingness to explore new interests.

Dialogue with Dave: Excerpt A
Present: MD (Mike Duane), PK (Pat Kitto), DK (Dick Kitto).

MD: I came up several times last year/ and I myself noticed that as the year went on/ so you and the others got more confident/ you were able to argue with Dick and Pat and Ken and Neal/ in a way which you weren't able to do at the beginning/ um/ would you feel that's/ that what I'm saying, is true is right/ did you experience did you feel yourself/ that as the year went on/ you felt more able to argue like this and put your point of view?

Dave: I did/ at the beginning it were like/ like at school you know/ you'd like to argue/ 'cos at school you couldn't argue wi' teachers.

MD: Yes/ did you see Dick and Pat and the others more as teachers than anything?

Dave: Yeh/ and they/ y'know when we sort of started/ to get to know them/ well we you know/ you just started to talk to them normal/ and/ y'know you're working wi' em and you see 'em every day/ so you talk to them normal.

MD: Can you remember/ sort of/ what it was, or can you remember any particular case in which/ something they said or something they did suddenly made you think/ 'Cor they're not ordinary teachers'/ or did it grow gradually?

Dave (without hesitation): It just grew gradual.

MD: I was wondering whether some of those early discussions in which you sat around/ in that room/ and you know, people said 'Well, what would you like to do and we could so this, we could do that, what would you like to do?' / whether you felt that that was rather different from the usual classroom situation?

Dave: Yes you had a choice of what you wanted to do/ you know if I like doing canoeing we could go canoeing/ we didn't have to stick to a schedule like we did at school.

MD: Had you found at school that teachers had sometimes said 'What would you like to do' / at all or not/ did you never experience anything like this at school at all?

Dave: In Outward Bound we'd say/ 'can we go canoeing/ or rock-climbing' and then they'd say/ 'We can't go rock-climbing this week because they've took all rock-climbing things away, we can't go canoeing because all canoes are bust'/ so we never did it.

MD: I see/ yes yes/ so you felt that although we were invited to make suggestions nothing ever came of them/ whereas here/ you made suggestions and you could do something about it/ (substantial pause)/ Suppose someone asked you to sort of look back and say what were the important things that happened/ for you during the year what would you/ what would spring to mind most quickly?

Dave (long pause – three seconds): I think it's just being friends/ y'know wi'/ wi' kids that were 'ere/ who I'd never known before at school y'know/ I'd just say 'Ay oop' to them at school/ and then you'd find out that they were really good mates wi' yer/ and you'd had really good relationships wi' everybody down here.

MD: I mean they actually had been in your same class at school/ had they?

Dave: We were in different forms so we never came into contact with them.

MD: You didn't really meet them/ yeh/ but some of those down here had been in the same form as you had they/ did you find that even so they/ you had a different relationship with them down here?

Dave: See/ when they were in the same form as me/ well I never had nowt to do wi' them and when they came down I never had nowt to do wi' them then.

MD: I see.

Dave: Y'know, I just went on to people I'd never known before.

MD: So the people who had been in your form at school/ when you met them down here you didn't make any sort of further friendship with them because they weren't the sort of people you wanted to be friends with/ but the people from different forms/ you suddenly found that these could be good friends and you made friends with them/ in a way which you couldn't do at school.

Dave (nods agreement).

MD: How did the um/ sort of work you were doing down here strike you?

Dave: *Great* (with emphasis)/ it were all practical/ y'know that's/ that's what I'm good at.

MD: You like that?

Dave: Yeh/ I like practical things/ it/ it were like, y'know summat/ I don't know it, it just got me inside/ y'know everything practical y'know/ I wanted to do it.

MD: But did you have practical work at school?

Dave: Yeh we had metalwork/ but then you had/ you had to be restricted again because you had to pay for metal/ and so you didn't like going home and saying 'Mum, I've just made a dressing table, it's going to cost you £5.95'/ and your mother would say 'Oh', y'know at having to pay it.

Commentary – Dave (Excerpt A)

'Argument', the proposing and justifying of alternative views, can be a powerful instrument for the sharpening of linguistic abilities: it is essential to the development of intelligent, rational and scientific thought.

Dave quite clearly feels that the opportunities for this type of activity were missing, or were limited, during his time at school (lines 1-10, 'cos at school you couldn't argue wi' teachers'. Why not?) So, by reaction, argument (first as a form of self-assertion) became a matter for exploration at The Terrace. From being a 'try-on' or a 'testing-out' it developed into something much more important. The real value of argument was not discovered until this stage had been gone through; that is, when students discovered that they could 'talk to [the teachers] normal' (page 47, lines 15-16).

Such an awareness very clearly depends on the type of relationship that exists between student and teacher. As we shall see in a number of transcriptions, the matter of relationships is very important to these lads; relationships among themselves and their peers as well as relationships with staff and other adults with whom they came into contact during their time at The Terrace. As a direct result of his course at The Terrace, Dave was able to fashion new perceptions of others whom he had previously not really bothered to get to know (see page 48 line 12 to page 49 line 3). Significantly, after a long pause, Dave's response to MD's question (page 48, lines 6-11) is 'I think it's just being friends'. This reply demonstrated a power of reflection and a judgement of experience extending over a period of ten months. Dave's answer goes to the heart of one of the most important intentions held by Royston Lambert and by the staff at The Terrace – the creation of personal bonds and personal involvement that would, it was hoped, lead to self-discipline, self-awareness and a widening of interest.

One important means of promoting this self-development is through participation in genuine decision-making. Page 47 line 22 to page 48 line 19 indicate something of this involvement. Dave's recognition of one of the institutional restrains imposed by schools (page 47, line 30, 'we didn't have to stick to a schedule like we did at school') points to one of the frustrations experienced by perhaps a good number of older schoolchildren. How *is* the school to allow for flexibility – to encourage involvement and development – and yet organise a structure which will respond to a range of demands?

For some students, and for Dave certainly, there is the need to be *active*; to be engaged in something productive. His response to MD's question (page 49, lines 4-5) is very clear. At this point the tape-recording catches the tone and volume of his words, but not the physical changes noted at the time. For facial expression and bodily movement here also indicate his feeling of enthusiasm ('great/ it were all practical/ y'know that's/ that's what I'm good at', lines 6-7). These words, together with the physical changes that went alongside his speech, perfectly conveyed to his listeners how deeply he had been moved by a situation in which he felt confident, in contrast to what he had previously expected of school. Dave's last response in this excerpt (lines 13-17) tells us something of his relationship with his mother – the simple matter of wishing to please her by showing the result of his skill – and the impact made on this by an economic consideration. The result, again, is that 'you had to be restricted' (page 49 line 13).

Page 47 lines 14-17: *well we you know/ you just started to talk to them as normal ...* – reformulation of idea. *Y'know you're working ...* – explanation to make clear why *you just started to talk to them normal.* Forms of address between persons always to some extent predicate the type of relationship it is possible to develop.

Page 47 line 22: *It just grew gradual ...* – the immediacy of this response evident on tape but not in typescript, indicates the speed with which Dave answered the question. He maintains his own dialectical form of the adverb where MD uses 'gradually'. Such maintenance could be seen as a rejection of MD's style, but in the context of the whole dialogue is much more likely to indicate relaxation and confidence that his own style is respected; especially since all the boys maintain their own speech styles.

Today, fortunately, more teachers are more sensitive to dialect and respect its speech forms – though one suspects that there is still some tendency to make the lad who wears 'kecks' at home wear 'trousers' at school. Perhaps there is here even a positive case to be made for the introduction of dialect material in schools: a wide range is now available (e.g. the BBC disc *Some British Accents and Dialects*, 1971, RESR 28M).

Dialogue with Dave: Excerpt B

MD: One thing that stuck in my mind/ I may have got this totally wrong/ and put me right/ I felt/ that the famous occasion on which you had a strike/ do you remember?

Dave: Yeh.

MD: When the boys went on strike/ I felt this was a very very important point in the year/ did you feel that?

Dave: It weren't really a strike were it? (smiling and in an amused tone)

MD: No no/ but I mean/ tell me in/ the way it occurred to you.

Dave: It were just/ *they* (emphatic) said/ they put it to'ards Neal that they wanted to try out a new system/ of work y'know/ wi' them Starcross girls coming up they wanted to try it out/ they did it really because they were getting sick of what they were doing on furniture/ and they just wanted a rest/ and so they said that/ 'What we'll do/ if you want to work you can work'/ but none of these were because they were sick of doing it/ and *I* (emphatic) was sick/ I were a big offender me/ 'cos I were saying to them 'We don't want to do work' and 'Don't do work'/ I never liked it anyway doing furniture/ I suppose *they* got something out of it.

DK: You never liked what?

Dave: Doing furniture.

DK: But you chose that as against going up to the allotment didn't you?

MD (laughs)

Dave: I know I took to

DK: Because you used to/ to start with you were very keen on the allotment/ and then eventually you reached a stage when you preferred to work down here than going up there.

Dave: That were because of Neal.

DK: Why?

Dave: Because I tried me best to do things/ for him y'know to try and improve it/ but every time I did something he used to get on at me a bit/ he used to say 'Pull it down' I'd build a fence and he'd say 'Pull it down it's no good'/ and so/ he kept going on/ and so I just/ that were it/ I jacked it in/ and so I came down here/ for what work I did on that furniture is/ that much (gestures with thumb and index finger)/ you know/ very small/ I just mucked around.

DK: Do you think you deteriorated after you left the allotment a little bit?

Dialogue with Dave

Dave: Yeh until/ until I found y'know/ I had Stringer's signposts to do (reference to contract for a local firm).

DK: Was that because you didn't get on with Ken at that time?

Dave: I just/ I never bothered with Ken/ I'd always liked Neal at school 'cos he used to teach me see in Humanities/ um/ you know he's a good laugh/ and so I just hung around Neal like/ but then when I found out how Ken were/ I just changed I went to Ken.

DK: It was all personality was it then?

Dave: Mmm/ it were just like kids around here y'know/ I liked Ian Hardy and Nelly and Alex so/ us four just hung around/ I just switched from people to people.

DK: Yeh/ do you think everyone does that?

Dave (shrugs shoulders)

MD: Did you find Ken made demands on you at first which/ you couldn't get on with/ you see one of the things Ken said at one point was that he found that when the time came to stop work/ the boys would just sort of/ go leaving everything as it stood tools glue whatever it was they'd just go/ and um/ this was a difficulty because obviously it meant that/ things had to be sorted out next morning when they started again/ or if he asked people to clear up put things away they'd sling things in the cupboard and push off/ what was your side of this situation was Ken making demands on you that you didn't think were reasonable at the time?

Dave: No/ that it were just that everybody wanted to get home I suppose/ they just flung everything into cupboards and 'Let's get gone'/ it weren't a demand were it/ it were just that/ we just wanted to go/ and get out of the way.

MD: But um/ did the thought not cross your mind that/ well if the cupboard was full of a load of junk next morning you'd have to spend an awful lot of time sorting it out or was that something that didn't really matter?

Dave: It didn't matter because we didn't have to sort anything out/

we'd just pick it out of the cupboard/ and once we've used it leave it on bench/ and then it'd be there all day until four o'clock and then we'd throw it back in the cupboard.

MD: Were you then thinking that the demand of Ken or anybody else for that matter was making on you was a bit/ daft?

Dave: Yeh.

MD: There was no point in getting things all neatly organised because you were going to come back to it again next day?

Dave: Yeh right.

MD: How was the strike as I call it/ actually resolved how did it sort itself out/ who started the move to get things back to/ normal?

Dave: Well we had a week/ they said you could have a week of it/ have a try on.

MD: And what did you do during that week?

Dave: We played cards and

MD: Brewed tea

Dave: And that's all we did all week and it were getting into a mess/ you know and Neal and Ken/ especially Ken 'cos he made it the Coach House/ he were getting mad about it/ he said 'You don't really care about this place'/ *we do you know* (with show of feeling) but/ we'd clear it away and then we'd come back in and we'd start playing cards and it would get into a mess again/ and then Ken would just walk in at that moment when it were in a mess/ and when that strike were on it were/ I kept shouting at Neal and Ken because they didn't side wi' us/ they called it a strike and we called it a test/ testing this new education out.

MD (laughs loud and long – joined by DK): What was it you were testing?

Dave: We just wanted to see what it were like just sitting around.

MD: I see.

Dialogue with Dave

Dave: But they said all we wanted to do was skive from work which we wanted to do.

MD: But they also said? 'It's your decision'/ and you wanted to test them out whether it really was your decision.

Dave (laughs): We weren't testing them out to see whether it were *our* (emphatic) decision.

MD: Well were you testing them out to see if they really meant what they said?

Dave (immediate response): *Yeh* that's what we wanted to know.

PK: And do you think they did?

Dave: Mmm/ Neal did but Ken didn't/ Ken didn't want us to stop work because he said they were in financial/ financial difficulties and we said 'Well we can stop work for a week'/ Ken said 'But we can't'/ and Neal says 'If they want to laze around all week let them'.

PK: That was quite true actually Neal in a way accepted it/ it wasn't that Ken didn't accept it it was that Ken couldn't he really did feel very involved in the place.

DK: He felt that it was a personal affront to him.

PK: It was much more an emotional thing than anything.

DK: Don't you like it? (offering glass of wine to Dave)

Dave: I've not tried it yet.

MD: Well this is a point which is very important to me/ Ken was concerned that the finances might get into a jam/ or do you think that Ken would become very anxious/ just because people were idle?

Dave: He just didn't like us sitting around.

MD: Doing nothing/ that upset him.

Dave: And making place untidy/ 'cos he played a big part in making that Coach House.

MD: So in a sense you were/ spoiling his handiwork?

Dave: Yes/ he didn't like us sitting around because we were making a lot of mess and we'd made it y'know/ we'd made the mess and we'd made the Coach House/ it just *seemed* (emphatic) that we didn't care about it any more.

MD: Well now/ why do you think Neal didn't get uptight about this?

Dave: Because I think that Neal never you know/ he were never there to see Coach House constructed/ he were always up on allotment.

MD: I see/ so in a sense it wasn't his baby/ in the same way that it was Ken's baby/ (lengthy pause) did you ever talk to Royston?

Dave: Yeh.

MD: Did he ever tell you the story about the boys and the fathers in Africa of a certain tribe/ who when they start their apprenticeship/ build the building in which they are going to do the work/ and produce the equipment and so on/ and they then go through their training apprenticeship or whatever it is/ and when they've finished they set fire to the lot/ burn it right down to the ground/ did he ever tell you about that?

Dave: No.

MD: That seemed to me a great story because er/ it means then that every new generation of boys who are going to go through an apprenticeship have to really set to and build the whole thing up from scratch/ the way in which you in the first year were beginning to do here/ would that he a good idea do you think/ that every new generation of boys doing the ROSLA or girls doing the ROSLA/ should have to start from where you did/ more or less from scratch.

Dave: Yeh because then/ they'd realise that you know they've got to look after it 'cos they'd built it/ y'know I mean you won't go smashing it up if you'd built it/ like at school/ you knew that it were all school pencils and books so you didn't care about it you just ripped 'em up and broke pencils and carved your name in desk/ but if you had sanded desk and made and waxed it you wouldn't carve your name in it.

Commentary – Dave (Excerpt B)

In this long extract several important themes emerge. First, there is the matter of the 'strike' – a very significant testing-point of the scheme, of the teachers and, above all, the boys themselves. There is no doubt that through this experience the boys developed a new range of awareness of themselves and others.

Interspersing that debate is, again, the matter of personal relationships, especially as they are precipitated by the *need to make decisions*. These decisions, at one level, are to do with the running of The Terrace, the organisation of affairs. At another level, however, they are to do with a clash of attitudes. For the teachers, almost inevitably, there was a sense that some things were to be done not merely for what they were in themselves, but for the 'character-training' which they would help to promote. For the boys these things were weighed purely pragmatically. The sort of pragmatism we see here is exactly that to which Richard Hoggart, in *The Uses of Literacy*, makes frequent reference among the working classes.* Though a testing-time there is no doubt that the outcome of this clash between principles and pragmatism was genuinely productive. Dave sees quite clearly, for instance, the 'other point of view' – even though he is not persuaded by it. Throughout these dialogues there is ample evidence that principles do not in themselves determine courses of action in advance of a situation: rather that the specific nature of each situation determines the relevance of the principle. 'What is appropriate' is more convincing that 'what is right'.

---

* e.g. 'It will be useful first to recall that group of attitudes which includes an unidealistic tolerance, a pragmatism, a taking-life-as-it-comes, a goodwill-humanism, a dislike of objecting on principle (rather than for clear and recognisably 'human' reasons). There are some things no decent person would do, it is assumed, and they are fairly easily known. If judgement seems to be invited on much more, then the suspicion of 'moral talk' (which can obviously have a healthy future) comes into play, and there is a switching-over to an appropriate, blurring counter – 'Y've got to live and let live'; almost anything is 'alright in its place'; 'it doesn't matter what y' believe so long as yer heart's in the right place'; and 'it wouldn't do for us all to think alike'.' – *The Uses of Literacy*, Penguin, 1958, page 142.

Yet this qualification, as Dave demonstrated, does not mean that 'social lessons' are inaccessible or cannot be learned. Quite the reverse, in fact, is demonstrated by Dave's reply (page 56 lines 26-32) to MD's account (page 56 lines 11-25) of the story told by Royston Lambert. For Dave here switches the significance of the fable to an immediate social context. The point is not 'lost' – it is *applied*, and with a perceptive sureness. Morality may be 'out there': but social reality is very much present.

Page 51 line 32: 'It weren't really a strike ...' – Dave corrects the impression of the adults, and in so doing initiates an important post-mortem on the event and its experiences.

Page 52 lines 2-11: Throughout this statement Dave maintains a contrast between himself and the rest of the group by emphasising *they* (line 2) and, seven lines later, emphasising *I*. The contrast relates to a) the fact that it was the others, not Dave, who approached Neal, and b) their attitude to working on the furniture. This contrast, now focusing on interest in the work, is picked up again and underlined by the emphasis in the final *they* (ten lines after the initial distinction).

The statement is complicated by a number of parenthical references. The first of these refers to the Starcross girls. A group of girls from Starcross School in Islington had been invited to spend a few days at The Terrace as part of their own programme for widening their experience. They had shocked the boys with their language and by their suggestion that the boys were allowing themselves to be pushed around too easily. They thought the work being done by the boys was dirty and unnecessary and they urged them to take it easy.

Dave knows that the adults are aware of this visit and does not, at this point, refer to the girls' behaviour or the arguments they used.

The second parenthical reference points to another reason for the boys' wish 'to try out a new system of work' – simply the fact that they were 'getting sick' of it and wanted a rest.

The third statement is a frank confession that he himself 'were a big offender' in urging the others to stop because he had never got anything out of it.

The exchanges that follow with Dick reveal that his attitude to work had in fact been very different from what Dick had supposed (Dick's own upbringing had been – public school, the Navy and then on the staff of Dartington School).

Page 52 lines 21-29: Here Dave makes clear the clash of personalities between himself and the teacher who, to Dave at least, appeared somewhat of a perfectionist – and thus unreasonable in the demands he made of the lad. 'I tried me best to do things' carries a convincing tone. At a certain point, then, he could no longer accept the teacher's criticism. He had reached his own limit – 'that were it' is said with the utter finality which signifies breakdown. The rest of Dave's 'confession' – for such it is – honestly admits to his reactions when he gave up working on the allotment.

Page 52 line 30: Dave takes in his stride Dick's word 'deteriorated' and responds appropriately. Dave, however, is neither uncritical nor unchallenging of words – as shown in the next excerpt.

Page 53 lines 4-13: Dave expresses his own awareness of the differences in personality between Ken and Neal. At school he had been attracted to Neal because he was 'a good laugh'; in the new 'work situation' at The Terrace, however, he discovered Ken to be more compatible. Prompted by Dick to generalise from this experience – 'do you think everyone does that?' – Dave shrugs his shoulders. Such a non-committal gesture is a specific reinforcement of what Richard Hoggart referred to as 'unidealistic tolerance'; Dave will speak of what he can specifically identify, like his own relationship with Ian, Nelly and Alex – but he will not be drawn to act as spokesman for people outside his own experience.

Page 53 line 14 to page 54 line 7: This long exchange poses, through an actual situation, the clash between the boys' pragmatic view of things and that view, of the same undertaking, which sees order and discipline and rules and regulations as necessary to the accomplishment of any given task. To MD's suggestion (lines 22-23) that the boys were reacting against the unreasonableness of Ken's demands for doing things in an organised way, Dave offers a more obvious reason: 'everybody wanted to get home'. To MD's pressing of the matter (lines 28-31) Dave's answer is equally functional and pragmatic – the way of doing things is the way that works for those doing the work, however distressing to anyone else who tries to organise the way of working for them. There is reinforcement when Dave then agrees with MD's suggestion that Ken's demand for tidiness was unnecessary, 'daft'. Dave's emphatic agreement – 'yeh right' (page 54 line 9) – is further confirmation.

Page 54 line 10: MD returns to the matter of the 'strike' with which the extract opened. The whole of the dialogue from page 52 line 12 (Dick's interjection) up to this point can thus be seen as an exploration of matters raised almost incidentally. Tangential to discussion proper of the 'strike', the talk has largely focused on the question of relationships. Significantly it is Dick, through his questions (seven in all, and one statement) who is responsible for the direction of this part of the talk; having been intimately connected with The Terrace and the boys he is still puzzling over fairly immediate experience – and it is *his* attempt to come to terms with personality shifts and relationships which gives impetus.

Page 54 lines 12-13: The significance (for Dave) of the nature of the week's 'try-on', a nature evidently misunderstood by adults at the time, as now, becomes the subject of enquiry for much of the rest of the dialogue, enabling also a return to consideration of personalities as revealed, to Dave, throughout that time.

Page 54 lines 17-26: This lengthy statement makes clear that the 'strike' was in fact a test – 'testing this new education out' – of the sincerity of the adults and of the whole Terrace scheme. The boys had been told that the scheme would be controlled democratically by the group, and they were putting to the test this resolution.

The conflict, as we have seen in previous exchanges, was also about the attempt to instil 'character-training' (Ken's demands for tidiness and order) and the boys' thoroughly functional approach. Now, however, Dave makes clear that he is sensitive to the fact that Ken had invested a good deal of personal commitment to The Terrace scheme and its success. He had been very much involved in making the Coach House in the first place, and Dave appreciates Ken's reactions. He understands them, but equally wants his own motives to be understood. Such lack of understanding is fully expressed by Dave: 'They called it a strike and we called it a test'. In eleven words

Dialogue with Dave

the cause of the confusion is made quite clear.

Dave also makes it clear that the boys *are* concerned about the scheme: 'we do you know' – a parenthesis aimed at his present listeners – is spoken with great feeling. Significantly his present-tense indicates that he still feels involved; his presence alone, months after he had left school and The Terrace scheme, seems support for such a reading.

Page 55 line 12: 'Which we wanted to do.' Dave readily admits that the boys also did want to 'skive from work'.

Page 55 lines 5-19: 'We weren't testing ... decision.' Dave is clear about the precise reason for the test and confirms this by his emphatic and immediate response in line 9 to MD's suggestion that they were testing the sincerity of the *staff*. Dave is also very much aware of the difference between Ken and Neal in the matter of commitment to the scheme. Dave's perception of these differences is immediately confirmed by Pat and Dick in lines 15-19.

Page 55 line 22 to page 56 line 7: Dave is aware than Ken was upset for a number of reasons: 'he just didn't like us sitting around'; 'making place untidy'; generally upsetting his plans. Dave recognises Ken's personal involvement – 'he played a big part in making that Coach House' – but, as he sees it, because the boys themselves had been largely responsible for doing the work, they were also 'entitled' to make a mess in it if they chose to. The significance of these remarks is further defined later in the dialogue. Dave is saying, therefore, that their actions at the time were misinterpreted – 'it just seemed [i.e. to Ken] that we didn't care about it any more'. Read in conjunction with Dave's earlier emphatic expression of involvement ('we do you know') it is clear that the goings-on in the Coach House were indeed a test of the staff's commitment to the ideal of corporate decision-making, *not* a statement of the boys' lack of interest in the scheme. Similarly, Dave understands Neal's lack of concern (to the degree shown by Ken): 'he were never there to see Coach House constructed' (page 56 lines 6-7).

Page 56 lines 11-32: Dave's grasp of the implications of the story told by Royston Lambert is immediate, as in his perception of the development of the story as expressed by MD. His illustrations make this evident: 'they'd realise that you knew they've got to look after it 'cos they'd built it ...' Dave's final comment ('but if you had sanded desk and made and waxed it you wouldn't carve your name in it') illustrates, through precise and concrete example, a perfectly-conceived relation of Royston's 'moral fable'. It suggests also the accessibility of 'morality' when couched in fable form – taking us back to the tradition of Christ's parables, and beyond – as opposed to the bland (and *unattached*) prescription of generalised principles. There is, after all, no necessary connection between abstract principle and particular situation – since somewhere in our evaluation of experience the particularities of circumstance must be taken into account if we are to arrive at equable judgement.

Part IV
Some evidence and some conclusions

In the spring of 1975 I discussed the Conisbrough experiment with Ken, then working in the Research Unit at Dartington, set up by Royston Lambert to examine ROSLA schemes all over the country. I suggested to him that the scheme had been successful for eight main reasons that interlocked:

a) that there was an unusually high staff/student ratio as compared with what the students had previously experienced;

b) that there was an emphasis on practical work within the competence of the students;

c) that the students had been paid for their work;

d) that the scheme had brought them into contact with people other than teachers;

e) that control of the group was exercised democratically;

f) that they were free of the more petty restrictions of school;

g) that they were away from those teachers who rated their behaviour and their academic potential very low;

h) that they were in continuous contact with supportive adults.

In a letter to me after this meeting he wrote:

'The scheme did contain the various factors you have outlined in your notes, but many interventionist alternatives contain such factors as close adult relations, democratic organisation, high staff ratios, etc., and most schemes still remain highly stigmatising and reinforcing experiences (i.e. of old habits) ... physical separation ... is not nearly enough to explain what occurred. The failure of the old approved school treatment situation, which is generally, to say the least, isolated from the community, is enough to blast the theory of physical removal from one's cultural context as the key issue in social reorientation ...

I suspect the success of the 73/74 ROSLA experiment has got something to do with the ability and willingness of the children to weigh up the viability of the newly offered social orientation in comparison with the old. One only changes and adopts a new role when one is assured of the goods, the gratification, etc., otherwise one uses the situation to reinforce what one already has ...'

But the comparison by Ken of the separation of The Terrace with the separation of an approved school seems to miss the essential differences, such as that:

a) the ROSLA students were not detained against their will – though some pressure may have been applied, most volunteered for the scheme;

b) consistent truancy or misbehaviour would result, not in even more isolation or punishment, but simply in a return to school;

c) The Terrace was not set apart from the local culture – it was in the heart of that culture and parents and friends were welcomed – visits to an approved school are strictly rationed by the authority;

d) the stigma attached to an approved school certainly did not attach to The Terrace.

Of course physical separation from the school is effective only in so far as it also symbolises psychological separation from everything that school has come to represent in the minds of the ROSLA students. Students who know that they are regarded as failures and who are reminded daily that they are the 'duds' associate school books, school equipment, the very buildings and even the smell of school with rejection. No wonder that minor vandalism is so often seen to be the work of such students. Physical separation *can*, at one stroke, though it does not always do so, remove the people and the environment that, for these students, are saturated with an aura of disapproval and, too often, contempt.

Evidence of progress from the staff of The Terrace

Neal, a teacher from Northcliffe School, who had taught many of the boys on ROSLA I before the scheme had started, was himself born and bred in Conisbrough. He was therefore much closer to the boys in terms of understanding local culture and of understanding and sympathising with many of their reactions during the scheme. He had been keen to take part in the scheme and was confident that it would work, even against considerable discouragement from older and senior members of staff. As time went on he became even more enthusiastic and consistently praised and encouraged the boys even when their standards were lower than they could have been.

It was something of this that caused a rift to occur between Neal and Dick as the scheme progressed. Neal kept a very full diary of events and reactions and would have wished to carry on with ROSLA II but that he sensed that the differences with Dick were too great easily to be overcome and that he had, as the last term of ROSLA I drew to a close, begun to realise that both the LEA and the Dartington Hall Trustees would withdraw their support in face of mounting financial difficulties. He therefore decided to embark on what he had long wanted to do – a stay abroad for a few years.

In a recorded discussion he said:

'After The Terrace I'd never settle down easily again in an ordinary classroom. The Terrace was fantastic – close contact with the boys, plenty of practical work and a bunch of real keen people [staff] to work with. The changes in those boys was incredible. I knew most of them before, as I knew most of their friends who were not at The Terrace. The difference between The Terrace group and the others became more and more obvious as the year went on. Even in the first term The Terrace group were beginning to look on their old mates as just kids, behaviour-wise.

And in other ways, too, they seemed to mature faster than their old mates. They took more care of themselves – and not just to impress girls – they all do that at weekends or on special occasions – they looked cleaner; their clothes, even their working clothes, looked better cared for.

We should really have started something like this much sooner and while the boys are in the fourth or even second year. It would prevent a lot of sour feeling that gets into many of the boys as they get near to leaving school.'

Other evidence from The Terrace staff can be seen in Ken's report and in Pat Kitto's projected book about her experience at The Terrace.

From other staff of Northcliffe School

A metalwork master at the school:
'I was not very keen on this ROSLA scheme – really because only one of the team was a trained teacher and none of the others knew our boys, but I was prepared to give it a go. I didn't see much of the boys except when they came up to the workshop to do some welding or to borrow some tools. They seemed quieter, less inclined to act the goat as they often did. They seemed to listen more carefully when I was giving them instructions about using the equipment, and I felt that I could more easily leave them to get on with a job.

I suppose this would happen anyway. They were coming to see me in pairs or individually – not in a group of fifteen or sixteen like the ordinary classes.

Did I find them intelligent? I didn't notice all that much difference from before. If the boys are interested they will take notice and act intelligently.'

A young woman teacher at the school:
'I see them only when I come down to The Terrace. They always seem cheerful and polite to me; they are obviously enjoying being there and working with Dick – they are so enthusiastic if you ask them anything about The Terrace.

The atmosphere at The Terrace is so different from school. Northcliffe is, I would say, a good school so far as that goes, with pleasant, easy relationships between many of the staff, especially the younger ones and the newcomers, and the children. It's even better with the younger children in the first two or even three years. Betty [the woman deputy], Dave, Stewart, Bruce and two or three others have got the Featherstone Castle expedition going now as a regular thing. That starts the first year off well and it seems to continue back at school.

The oldest two years are not so amenable, especially those who are commonly spoken of as 'dim' or 'thick' by some of the older staff. They are usually rather more difficult to teach – they don't like academic work; they are easily distracted and they muck about at the slightest chance.

The Terrace boys now seem older, more mature, somehow. It may be because Pat and Dick don't treat them as most teachers do. They treat them as they do the Dartington students.'

A Northcliffe teacher, later appointed to the Dartington staff:
'The Terrace is really great. I've never known anything so good since I've been teaching. The kids are so alive compared to their friends still in the school.

What do I think are the main reasons for it? Well, obviously, there is far more personal contact between staff and kids than you can get in the normal class. The kids have a real say in what happens – and that you just don't see in school; I've never seen it in any school that I've known.

Another reason is that the work done is not only practical rather than academic, but it is real work – the kids do jobs such as decorating or repairing furniture – for which they are paid. The fact that the staff work alongside them in the same jobs, rather than sitting at the front and not soiling their hands, gives them a feeling of real co-operation. It also sets a practical example which can be – and often has been – criticised by the boys.

I know that some of the staff are not very happy about the scheme – but so far no one has been able to deny that the kids' attendance is fantastic, even compared with the A streams. Some staff try to brush even that off by saying that the whole scheme is just a skive anyway, but as the year has gone on they keep more quiet.

At the end of the first term, when the boys had performed their play in school and at the junior schools, the Head was as chuffed as a dog with two tails. Publicity seems to mean a lot to him and the scheme really got it.

I've talked to a lot of parents of boys in the lower streams – officially we don't have streaming but it seems to exist all the same. Most of them agree with me; they like the scheme and they say their boys have changed quite a bit. A few don't want to know. They just want to get the boys out to work – they'd have had them working at 12 or 13 if they'd had their way.

From parents

Neil's parents spoke with great feeling about the changes in their son 'Nelly':
'That's a grand scheme – the best thing that's happened here for a long time. Neil was right cheesed off with school until that last year.

Then he bucked up a lot. He'd never talked about school since he were quite a young boy, but when he got down to Terrace he were full of it, never heard him talk so much. And no more skiving off from school. His mother and me used to be worried in case he got into real trouble. Belting him seemed to do no good. I used to warn him that he wouldn't get a job if he didn't get a good report from school, but he didn't seem bothered.

Then all that stopped. We were right relieved I can tell you. Now he can talk to you like a man about jobs and that. Seems more interested in what's happening. He even reads the papers now.

Me – I were never that fond of school, but after a while I realised that if I'd paid more attention at school I could have got a different type of work, so I used to try and make Neil work harder. It weren't much good, though; he thought of nothing but football with the other lads.'

Pat Downing – parent and face worker in the local pit, Denaby Main:

'Education for ordinary lads and lasses is useless. They can pick up what they need to know in the jobs that they get round here. It doesn't give them any chance to get away from Conisbrough. My own lad would have been stuck here if Dartington hadn't offered him a place there. Now he's at a teacher-training college and loving it.

How many people would stay in Conisbrough if they got the education to go elsewhere? They *have* to keep us bloody stupid, else we wouldn't go down pit – not even for a hundred pound a week [spoken in 1974].

Dartington's doing a marvellous job here with this ROSLA scheme. The lads are getting plenty of help – they never got that at school. You can't always blame the teachers; they have too many to deal with and some of them are right tearaways.

You can talk to these lads at Terrace like young men. They're not boys any more. They think about what they are going to do and they're a bit more choosy, as they should be. Oh I know one or two of them haven't changed a lot, but that's the families they come from; they don't encourage them to make the best of it. If I had my way every lad and lass in school would have something like this – and not leave it to the last year in school.'

A Youth Employment Officer
'I interview most of the boys from Northcliffe School and from other schools in this area. Nearly all the boys at The Terrace have an alertness, a poise, a confidence in themselves and an openness towards the interviewer that stands out among boys who are classified by their schools as these boys were.

One can tell at once – however kindly the intention of the Head or his staff in the wording of their reports – that certain boys are expected to take their place in unskilled, routine or undemanding jobs. Very few boys in the lower streams of modern, or rather comprehensive, schools are given reports that encourage one to seek out something different, something more demanding for them.

But The Terrace boys have an air – I think it comes from the kinds of questions they ask – of having seriously thought not only about the job, but about their own qualities and resources in relation to the job.'

Visitors
An American visitor, himself a teacher and trainer of teachers, from Newton, Massachusetts:
'I have been in many English schools of all kinds since you raised the school leaving age. I've recognised an apathy of the kind we saw in our ghetto schools – mostly among students supposed to be non-academic. These kids here [The Terrace] look you in the eye; they talk freely; they are real interested in what you have to say; they like their work and show you round with pride; they speak of their teachers as friends and co-workers. That's good! That's real good!'

A lecturer from Derby College of Further Education:
'You said earlier that these students had been selected because they were in the lowest quarter of the academic range at their school. But having heard them talk of their experiences, both on this scheme and in their normal school, I am convinced that the assessment of their intelligence and their ability was grossly mistaken. They speak directly, even bluntly and in a strong South Yorkshire dialect, but the content of what they express and the relevance of their comments and their judgements puts them, in my view, certainly at an average level – and I have been teaching for nearly ten years with students from a similar background in a mining community.'

Criteria of effectiveness

I started with the assumption that if The Terrace educated the ROSLA students more effectively than their school had done, then this improvement would be reflected in a number of changes in their overall behaviour, and that the main problems in assessing the degree of improvement would lie in detecting and measuring improvement that could be seen to have arisen from the specific experience of The Terrace rather than from increased age and experience.

From the study that I am already pursuing into the meaning and effects of progressive education I had drawn up a number of criteria and had applied them tentatively to the progressive schools with which I was already familiar – Summerhill, Dartington, Monkton Wyld, Kilquhanity and Frensham Heights. These criteria were grouped under the following approximate headings – approximate because it is clear that many of the categories overlap. For example, effective use of language clearly associates with effective intelligence over a wide area, especially in the academic studies associated with school.

Linguistic competence:
Linguistic competence would be seen in a growth in both the active and the recognition vocabulary and range of grammatical structures; an increase in the ability to express more complex ideas in longer statements where appropriate; a greater skill in switching to elaborated code type statements where necessary; a finer sensitivity to variations of meaning in the use of different words and structures; and more sensitivity to variations in pitch, tone, emphasis and the whole range of body gestures.

Intelligence:
Increase in intelligence should be manifested in better performance in standardised intelligence tests (not applicable because these students had had no previous tests and since HM refused to allow them to undergo such tests); more effective solutions of everyday problems resulting from more concentration, more interest and more thought during the solution; a greater willingness to seek advice before taking action or when action was seen to be ineffective; more perseverance in the face of difficulty.

Disciplined behaviour:
An improvement in behaviour should be seen in a reduction in thoughtlessness and wilful damage to buildings, equipment, books, etc.; more care in executing work such as setting out tables for meals, cleaning rooms after use, cleaning and storing tools and materials to be used by others; greater self-restraint in group discussion and more consideration for the views and needs of others; more sensitivity in voice modulation according to circumstances.

Self-regard:
A heightening in self-regard should appear in more pride in personal appearance, such as in dressing with more care, taking more care of clothes, being cleaner and better groomed; dressing or using make-up more appropriately; walking and moving more freely and with more co-ordination.

Social awareness:
This should show itself in more interest in local, national and world events; more active participation in local activities, social work, youth activities, sport, other leisure activities; more curiosity about how the local community 'ticks'.

Personal responsiveness:
Personal responsiveness will be shown in more spontaneity in expressing sorrow, joy, love, hatred, sympathy, aversion; more sensitivity in detecting those feelings in others; greater freedom in appropriate bodily gesture and contact with others; greater sensitivity in attuning their own expressions and language so as not to cause unnecessary suffering to others.

ROSLA I

Taking these criteria as measures of the effectiveness of the ROSLA scheme it is clear that, in the view of those who took part in the scheme and of those who observed it – staff, parents, observers and students – the scheme worked: it did what it set out to do. When one compares Royston Lambert's plans for the scheme with the actual implementation of the scheme, at least during ROSLA I, it is clear that the team at The Terrace kept very close to the spirit and the letter of those plans. Where they departed from the plans, as in not using The Terrace as fully as possible for residence for the ROSLA groups, it was not that they objected in principle but that strong local tradition made staying away from home a thing not normally to be done.

More subtle changes appeared in their own awareness of themselves and of differences that had appeared during the scheme. Perhaps the most important of these changes were revealed in their language. The transcripts and the analysis of some dialogues reveal that their linguistic capacities are far in excess of what the school estimated them to be and in excess of their academic performance in school. It would be rash to claim that the ROSLA scheme *created* linguistic capacity in the students de novo, but in view of the confidence that appeared in their relationships with adults in an environment with radically different assumptions about their potential, it might rather be claimed that existing capacities were released by conditions that accorded the students simple respect.

Even though Northcliffe School is quite unusual among schools of that type, it cannot escape from the restrictions imposed by large classes and by educational assumptions springing from a different social-class basis. John Dewey wrote of the schools of his time as 'erecting silence into a virtue' and although many infant and junior schools have moved away from that kind of rigidity, far too many secondary schools have not. The imposition of silence in education denies not only the validity of the students' central human quality – speech – it denies everything that has been discovered over the last fifty years about the function of speech in perceiving and shaping reality for the individual.

For the ROSLA students such denial had been operating for ten years before the scheme started. It was not, therefore, surprising that the early weeks of ROSLA I were marked by suspicion of the motives of the staff, by apathy and by lack of co-operation. Refusal to talk, monosyllabic responses to direct questions, grunts or shrugs were typical of that period. Alternatively the adults were 'put down' by the boys making sly jokes to one another, smoking openly and keeping their overcoats on indoors as an indication of non-commitment; or simply by absenting themselves.

Such behaviour told its own sad story of the failure of their old schools to educate while it provided clear and bitter evidence of the function of schools for the working class in a class-dominated society.

'Society' needs some of its members to be the 'dumb oxen': schools, by devising curricula unrelated to life, by setting academic standards of performance that are meaningless in terms of the work of the local community, by rating the majority as failures and, in terms of class sizes and personal relationships, treating the majority as a 'mob', create the expectation within themselves that they are failures and deserve little out of life.

The dramatic nature of the change was revealed by the reactions of the group of experienced teachers (studying for a Diploma in the University of Nottingham) who questioned five of the boys from ROSLA I for over two and a half hours about the scheme. They refused to believe that the boys had been chosen for the scheme because their school had no hope for any kind of academic success. They compared them with similar boys whom they had taught and spoke of them as being 'thoughtful', 'intelligent', 'careful', 'sensitive', and found that they understood complex ideas readily and responded effectively.

Later, in an attempt to get some independent opinions on the levels of ability among the boys (the school had kept no records of any tests of intelligence and would not permit such tests to be made), the transcript of a discussion with six of the boys on ROSLA I (of which the discussion with Dave was part) was given to twenty London teachers experienced in secondary schools and Further Education. They were asked, on the basis of the transcripts, to grade the boys as 'average', 'above average' or 'below average' in intelligence. Not a single teacher placed any boy below average in intelligence; all, including Tiger who had been categorised by his school as nearly ESN (Educationally Sub Normal), were placed in the average or above average grade. Three of the teachers considered that two of the boys would be capable, with some preparatory help, of undertaking more advanced work at polytechnic or university level. One boy has since applied successfully for a place at Ruskin College, Oxford. All who have so far been asked about trade union membership have stated either that they have joined their union or that they would when they were old enough.

ROSLA II

ROSLA II started under a series of very severe handicaps that presaged if not failure then a lower level of success than had been experienced with ROSLA I. Nevertheless, enough evidence of positive changes in the boys and girls appeared during the first term to suggest that the success of ROSLA I was not simply the result of a lucky combination of circumstances unrelated to the central intentions of the scheme.

In contrast to the apathetic reluctance of ROSLA I, ROSLA II started with enthusiasm. This was the fruit, at least in part, of the success of ROSLA I: the enthusiasm of that group for The Terrace and all it stood for was evident to all. Further, there were to be some girls in ROSLA II. This had the immediate effect, since attitudes about boy/girl relationships at The Terrace were those of Dartington rather than of Northcliffe, of increasing the level of excitement in the group and making control more difficult for the depleted staff.

A good staff/student ratio, from the evidence of the diaries of both groups and from the transcripts of their discussions, is crucial to the democratic process of arguing out all issues of discipline, of standards of work, of care for equipment, of care for and sensitivity to others, as it is for providing the personal attention to literacy and to creating situations in which their confidence can grow. This conclusion is not new: it was agreed by the boys from ROSLA I in their discussion with Diploma students at Nottingham University and it is evidently in accord with the practice of the independent private schools in this country, traditional or progressive.

So, although ROSLA II clearly improved in all respects, they did so to a lesser extent than ROSLA I. Even from the beginning of ROSLA II Pat and Dick were more occupied with students from Dartington than they had been for the first term of ROSLA I. This, along with the reduction of staff caused by the loss of Ken, effectively reduced the staff so that barely two-thirds of the time devoted during ROSLA I to individual sessions with pupils and prolonged discussion of problems of attitude and behaviour were available for ROSLA II. But when Pat and Dick left, the students had already gained enough confidence to take matters into their own hands: instead of continuing to do what they had done with the adults, they now concentrated on 'doing their own thing'. They certainly did not vandalise The Terrace or behave in a disorderly or boisterous fashion. They spent a great deal of time talking quietly in small groups or wandering off to do whatever took their fancy. JB spent more time ferreting and poaching quietly in the woods or continuing to care for the chickens. Jane and Liz spent long hours talking; Tex usually went with JB; Alan pottered about on the allotment and shared the care of the chickens with JB; Jean preferred to spend time at home entertaining the other girls and gossiping; Mick had got himself a series of small jobs and was off to the Army as soon as possible. They usually kept close to The Terrace. Often I arrived to find the house silent and assumed that they were all out, only to find them quietly chatting in what had been Pat and Dick's sitting room.

Gerry adopted what was the only practicable course in the absence of paid work, funds and the minibus; he spent long hours talking with them, taking as many as could be persuaded on trips by bus, encouraging them to read the papers and talk about the news, making every effort to find jobs for them or help them in applying for jobs. The school being preoccupied with the problems of new buildings being erected in and about the existing building and having to alter its programme from day to day to suit the needs of the builders, was, presumably, glad that Gerry and his group were causing no 'trouble' and so left them alone. The boys and girls realised quite clearly that they would be left in peace as long as they continued to make no fuss.

Conclusion

How then can one summarise the Conisbrough experiment? In the view of this writer it marks a critical breakthrough from the socially isolated experiments of Summerhill, pre-Royston Lambert Dartington, Kilquhanity, Monkton Wyld, Frensham, and the other more apparently radical but essentially more traditional progressive schools. By its acceptance of the fact that a group is educational to the extent that it is focused on productive work as the well-spring of culture and discipline, it is close to the theory of John Dewey and Marx and to the practice of Homer Lane and Makarenko or to the psycho-therapeutic practice of Henderson Hospital. By its welcoming of parents and the local community as necessary to the success of its work it is allied to the theory and practice of The First Street Free School, the Liverpool Free School, Bermondsey Lampost Free School, and White Lion Free School – though, to date, the theory and the practice of these schools, with the exception of The First

Street Free School and White Lion Free School, have been available only to those who have visited them. By its assumption that the behaviour of young people, however apparently wild or irrational, springs from the logic of how they themselves have been brought up and see the world, it coincides with the views of Bruno Bettelheim.

Why did the ROSLA scheme have to end? It is important to ask this question rather than the usual question asked of any educational venture that comes to an end – 'Why did it fail?' It ended because funds ran out: Dartington could no longer sustain an experiment that had cost so much to establish. It ended because although the West Riding under Sir Alec Clegg's enthusiasm had planned steadily to take over full responsibility for the ROSLA scheme, the South Yorkshire Authority (as it had become) was not enough impressed by its educational and social value to provide the necessary money to sustain it.

But the statement 'We cannot afford it', whether made by the Dartington Trustees, by the new LEA (Local Education Authority) or by any other LEA is a political statement couched in financial terms. It says, in effect, 'We are not ready for the children of the working classes to be treated like the children of the élite. We cannot contemplate the prospect of the widespread social change that would result from such assumptions realised on a national scale. We dare not even begin to move from the established forms of education and forms of authority because that would challenge the very structure of our society. Those who placed us in power would disapprove.'

And how right they are! If democracy is simply the process of according with the habits, the expectations and the conveniences of the masses (already conditioned by schooling to have a low regard for themselves and to demand little for the future) as well as the decision-makers, then that kind of democracy is as doomed as any species unable to adapt creatively to a new environment. Fortunately democracy rests on more substantial foundations – it has also to do with equality, justice and love. So, although we may, for the moment, have heard the last of The Terrace as we seemed in the past to have heard the last of The Little Commonwealth or the emancipation of women, the power to generate change continues to operate, not from criteria of material efficiency but from 'the bowels of compassion'.

THE RAVEN 10
ANARCHIST QUARTERLY

on Education

This issue includes

John Shotton
The Authoritarian Tradition in British Education

Zeb Korycinska
Education versus Schooling: the case for home learning

Lyn Olson
Education or Processing

John R. Doheny
Intellectuals the the Industrialisation of Education

TWO RAVENS ON EDUCATION
both issues are 96 pages, £3 each (post free) from Freedom Press

This issue includes

Michael Duane
The Seeds of its own Destruction or Education in Capitalist Britain

Tony Gibson
Sexual Freedom at All Ages

Alex Comfort
Delinquency

John A. Schumacher
Our Responsibility for the Future of Higher Education

On Education (2)

WORK, LANGUAGE AND EDUCATION IN THE INDUSTRIAL STATE

by

Michael Duane

"The nature of work in industrial society today is such that those who stop to think about it wonder why so many millions of otherwise sane people spend so much of their lives, apparently without complaint, at work over which they have no control and from which they derive no personal satisfaction beyond receiving a wage."

36 pages   ISBN 0 900384 59 X   £1.00

CHILDREN IN SOCIETY
A LIBERTARIAN CRITIQUE

by

Stephen Cullen

"In our society children are largely a silent group, whose needs and wants are entirely determined by adults ... Such an approach arises from a refusal to treat children as having equal status and rights as any adult."

43 pages   ISBN 0 900384 62 X   £1.20

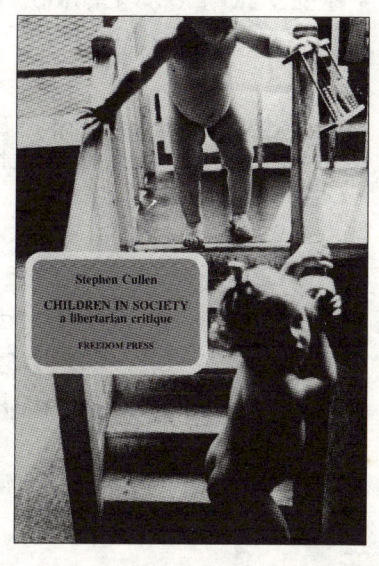

ABOUT FREEDOM PRESS

- FREEDOM PRESS are the publishers of the fortnightly journal *Freedom* and of the anarchist quarterly *The Raven*.

- FREEDOM PRESS are the publishers of books and pamphlets on anarchism and allied subjects. Our current list comprises some sixty titles.

- FREEDOM PRESS BOOKSHOP (open Monday to Saturday) carries a comprehensive stock of anarchist literature from this country, the USA and Canada. We also issue lists for the benefit of our mail order customers.

- FREEDOM PRESS DISTRIBUTORS are the European sales representatives for a number of small publishers in this country.

- This book has been printed by ALDGATE PRESS, a successful co-operative venture which also undertakes commercial printing work.

All particulars from
FREEDOM PRESS
84b Whitechapel High Street, London E1 7QX